LIENLORD

*The Complete Guide to Optimizing Your Investment
Portfolio With Secured Mortgage Loans*

Eric Scharaga

LIENLORD

Printed in the United States of America

First printing, 2020

Disclosure: Neither the author nor publisher are licensed financial advisors, attorneys, or CPAs, and are not giving financial, legal, or accounting advice in this book. The opinions expressed are the author's own and are based on his personal experiences and knowledge in alternative investments such as mortgage loans. Seek the advice of a competent financial advisor, attorney, and/or CPA who recognizes the value of alternative investments before making any financial, legal, or accounting decisions.

LIENLORD

For my amazing wife and children.

LIENLORD

Introduction

Alternative investments are becoming increasingly ubiquitous in the portfolios of investors all over the country. It's likely that by 2023, the global market for alternative investments will reach or exceed $14 trillion, with investors seeking a higher level of control and greater yields from this asset class.[1]

This information, while definitely compelling, comes as little shock to me. As I write this, the country is in the midst of the 2020 COVID-19 pandemic and resulting recession. As a result, we're seeing a lot of fear and turmoil surrounding the markets, where there was already a void in stable, low-risk, income-producing investments. Because of this, investors are left seeking yield in a falling bond market when more of them should consider turning to noncorrelated alternative investments.

Investors frequently look to real estate to provide fixed income solutions, many in retirement. What they learn, like I learned, is that rental property income is neither stable nor consistent. What if I told you that you could

---

[1] https://docs.preqin.com/reports/Preqin-Future-of-Alternatives-Report-October-2018.pdf

benefit from a *truly passive* real estate investment without all the headaches and risks?

It's difficult to sit on the sidelines, watching investors flounder when I know there's a better way. After all, I've been there myself. As a landlord, I struggled, which is what drove me to become a *lienlord*. This is my motivation for writing this book—to introduce more investors to the concept of becoming a lienlord by investing in secured mortgage loans.

Of course, this all starts with a question: *Why don't more investors consider mortgage loans as investments?* I don't see any reason why, other than lack of knowledge. It makes sense to avoid investing in something you don't know much about or don't understand. That's certainly what Warren Buffett suggests.[2] But here's the interesting point: If you have or have ever had a mortgage, then you know enough about mortgage investing to create a solid knowledge foundation. Hopefully, this book will round out that knowledge so you can determine whether mortgage loan investing is a suitable option for you.

> "Never invest in a business you cannot understand."
> —Warren Buffett

What Is Mortgage Loan Investing?

Investing in mortgage loans has provided me with a level of financial freedom I failed to achieve through my job and *two decades* of real estate investing. The numbers for the mortgage industry are staggering. As of 2019, there was

---

[2]https://www.cnbc.com/2017/05/01/7-insights-from-legendary-investor-warren-buffett.html

$15.8 trillion in mortgage debt in the United States.[3] Home ownership *is* the American dream, and you don't need to be a massive bank or financial institution to enjoy the benefits of mortgage loan investing. Everyday investors like us can invest in that dream.

When I purchase a residential mortgage loan as an investment, I am simply buying a debt obligation for a set number of payments from an existing loan that has already been originated, usually by a licensed financial institution. Once originated, the loan terms cannot be changed unless both parties agree. Originating mortgage loans is a completely different endeavor from buying and owning them. Origination is a tightly regulated business requiring licensure and compliance with myriad laws on the state and federal level.

Investors can buy the loans secured by multifamily properties, commercial properties, vacation homes, and single-family primary residences. For the purposes of this book, the focus will be on the latter—single-family, owner-occupied, primary residences—which I believe to be the safest mortgage-related investment.

Mortgage loans are *secured* loans, meaning that the borrower's home is pledged as collateral. A lien is recorded against the property to secure the lender's interest, and if the borrower ever defaults, the lender has the right to foreclose the collateral and sell the property in order to satisfy the debt.

While the borrower is the rightful owner of the property and is allowed all the rights and responsibilities of ownership, that ownership is subject to the lender's lien on the property, which must be paid in full before the borrower

---

[3]https://www.housingwire.com/articles/u-s-mortgage-debt-hits-a-record-15-8-trillion/

completely owns the home. What the borrower builds in the meantime is *equity*, or the difference between the value of the property and the amount of debt owed to the lender. Over time, equity grows as the value continues to rise and the amount of debt is paid back to the lender.

The types of loans covered in this book are referred to as *performing loans*, and there's a good reason for that. In a performing loan, the borrower is current and making regular payments. This is something that can help an investor feel confident about their investment, but I want to be clear that tracking billing and payments is not part of the job of a mortgage loan investor.

Almost all investors hire a *loan servicer* to manage their mortgage loans. Servicers are usually licensed in the states in which they service loans and charge a flat monthly fee per loan for servicing. This involves:

- notifying the borrower of any changes in loan ownership
- sending monthly mortgage statements
- collecting monthly payments
- keeping track of the payments and loan balance via payment history
- communicating with the borrower
- paying property taxes through an escrow account
- collecting proof of hazard insurance on the property
- disbursing monthly payments to the lender
- following up on any delinquencies
- handling payoffs
- sending out year-end tax statements to the borrower and lender

I use several servicers, and find that their monthly servicing fees range from $15 to $30 per month, per loan.

Considering the amount of work, regulation, licensure, and responsibility it takes to service a loan, this is a bargain. Part of the beauty of mortgage loan investing is that the lender has no other responsibilities for the collateral property; that is entirely up to the homeowner. Ultimately, mortgage loan investing is a simple business. Money was lent, the borrower needs to pay it back in monthly payments, the investor buys the lender's rights to the repayment, and the rest is an opportunity for our accounts to grow exponentially.

Feel free to contact me with any questions or for more information about mortgage loan investing.

Eric Scharaga
www.ericscharaga.com
eric@damencapital.com
847-222-8888

My Story: Seeking Freedom

I'm often asked what led me into mortgage loan investing, and I point to an incident that occurred when I was thirteen that really shaped my view of money.

I grew up the oldest child in a single-parent home in Hoffman Estates, a suburb about forty minutes northwest of Chicago. Hoffman Estates was where my family had our first home and first mortgage.

I was lucky enough to attend one of the top high schools in the state, filled with students split between my middle-class town and a much more affluent town next door. Many of my affluent friends' parents were executives, business owners, or doctors, and it was not uncommon for my friends to drive brand-new Porsches and Mercedes to school.

One day after riding my bike home from a baseball game, I saw my mom talking to a city inspector. Our main sewer line kept backing up, and the city inspector said that our only option was to hire a plumber to run a camera down the pipe and diagnose the problem. He pointed down to a section of our yard, right before the sidewalk, that was sunken.

"That's likely your problem there," he said. "If the crack is on the street side of the sidewalk, the village is responsible for the repair. But if the crack is on the homeowner's side, you'll have to repair it." He estimated the cost for the repair at $5,000 to $10,000.

I recognized the panicked look on my mom's face. I knew enough to know that we didn't have the money to pay for the repairs; my mom was a teacher, and we lived paycheck to paycheck my entire upbringing.

I felt totally helpless standing there next to her, with no knowledge of plumbing and no ability to get anywhere near the amount of money required to pay the repair bill. I grew frustrated with the situation, embarrassed, then angry, and made a silent vow to myself that day to never be in that position again.

From that point forward, for me, money represented freedom. Freedom from having to worry. Forget the material possessions; money meant complete control over my own life.

Ten years later, I found myself training to become a high school teacher in the same district I attended as a student. For twenty-three years, I went to work every day out of a sense of responsibility. I believed in the mission of public education in our society as the great leveler, and I believed I had a responsibility to inspire and guide my students, many of whom struggled at home.

But midcareer, I found myself struggling daily with the sheer weight of the profession. The days were long and intense, and the workload was never ending. I spent many days hiding an immense sense of frustration and feeling completely overwhelmed, seeing firsthand what my students had to struggle through.

Regularly, I came home from work and hid. All my energy was spent, and I had little to nothing left for my own children. I would get depressed and stressed out Sunday nights thinking about the week ahead. Honestly, there were many days that I would arrive in the parking lot and just sit there, not ready to get out of the car.

This is the problem too many people find themselves in, regardless of their profession. Stuck, too tired to figure a way out, and resigned to unhappiness. As a teacher, I learned that most of my coworkers felt like they had no choice but to stick it out for thirty-six years for the pension, the promise of future happiness.

During my quest for financial freedom, I invested in traditional investments and real estate, but nothing met my needs for stability, passive income, and scalability until I found mortgage loan investing in 2016. It represented everything that real estate investing wasn't.

By 2019, after twenty-three years of service, I retired from teaching. I entered into the great unknown of entrepreneurship with a wife and young kids who depended on me to provide for them. I knew it was time. I knew that if I stayed, I would regret being unhappy more than if I failed.

As of the date of this book, I have purchased over 250 mortgage loans. I am by no means rich, but I am financially self-sufficient, and I am able to support my family using my investment income, which was my original goal. Material possessions still don't matter to me. As I get older, the more I think about what I am building and what I am passing on to my children, in lessons and in legacy.

I am grateful for all the people I met in my early years in mortgage loan investing as well as my mentor, because they all taught me lessons that have turned me into the investor I am today. I am still learning about this business every day, and I enjoy passing on my knowledge to others.

I made a promise to my mentor early on in our relationship that in exchange for his help, I would teach someone else this business. I see this book as a means of fulfilling that promise, and sincerely hope you learn something valuable by reading it.

This book is not a complete educational program in mortgage loan investing; it is considered an introduction, designed to pique your interest and to make a case for a real estate-based, passive supplement to traditional investments.

I understand that not everyone will be as driven as I was for change, and most people are generally satisfied with their careers. But I believe there are many more investors who would choose mortgage investing for a part of their investment portfolio, because it is such a simple yet effective model.

I strongly believe that we all should have the opportunity to control our financial futures and create the lives we desire. Mortgage loan investing has allowed me to do that—I hope it can help you too.

The Real Estate Investing Myth

Since 2013, real estate has been the most popular investment in America.[4] Whether flipping, residential rentals, commercial rentals, or vacation rentals, real estate draws in investors like few other investments do. Many look to real estate to fulfill their dreams of passive investment income, when really, they should be looking at mortgage loan investing.

No matter what you've read in the countless real estate investing books available, owning real estate and renting it, for any reason, is not a passive investment unless you invest in a REIT, syndication, or fund. The thirteen years I spent as a landlord taught me that owning a rental property is the furthest thing from passive investment you can get.

Ironically, the number one candidate for mortgage loan investment is the burned-out landlord looking for a less stressful and more passive real estate investment

---

[4] https://news.gallup.com/poll/309233/stock-investments-lose-luster-covid-sell-off.aspx

option. Remember my experience as a child, standing in the front yard, overwhelmed by the cost of the massive repairs required in real estate ownership? That was merely an introduction of what was to come.

Becoming the Burned-Out Landlord

Real estate investment wasn't on my radar until 2001 when I read *Rich Dad, Poor Dad*. The book's message convinced me that the secret to financial freedom was cash flow obtainable through real estate investing: owning rental properties that would bring in stable monthly income.

Every real estate investing book I read told me that cash flow from real estate ownership was the number one path to wealth in America. I took that to heart and earnestly learned everything that I could about rental investing. I found a mentor who was an attorney, became a licensed real estate broker, and started my own single-person brokerage. I scaled a real estate business that allowed me to purchase and flip homes for profit while accumulating thirty-eight rental properties in the Chicagoland market.

Dream come true, right? **Wrong.** Because after thirteen years, my fantasy of leaving my teaching job and being financially free seemed even further away than when I was investing in mutual funds.

I learned the hard way that being a real estate investor was a grueling business, even more volatile than the stock market. There's an old expression in real estate: *You make your money when you buy, not when you sell.* Unfortunately, purchasing discounted properties was even harder than picking winning lottery numbers. The ever-growing number of real estate investors, many inexperienced, increased competition and drove up prices for properties to irrational levels. It was not uncommon for

18

discounted properties to have over thirty bids from investors. Rehabbing older properties revealed latent defects and hard-to-estimate expenses. Tenants were especially hard on the properties, and every tenant turnover cost an average of $5,000. This would include often-forgotten costs such as vacancy expenses and advertising for and finding a qualified tenant. I even hired several property management companies to help me with my business, only to see my problems, costs, and oversight increase.

The downturn of 2008 proved especially challenging. Many of my tenants lost their jobs and couldn't pay their rent. Spreading risk between more units failed to provide any type of hedge against loss; it just amplified the risk. As a landlord, I found there weren't really any laws working in my favor. Laws were overwhelmingly designed to protect tenants (and they should be), but they created an untenable model for me. Trying to create a stable, passive income from tenants who are frequently struggling from paycheck to paycheck in an environment that views landlords as the enemy isn't a practical business model.

Then there was the interpersonal aspect of the job. I've never met anyone who enjoys dealing with tenant drama, demands, excuses, and problems. I loathed it.

I tried everything I could to trim expenses and run a nimble business, but in thirteen years, I never made anywhere near what I projected. I could not support my family as a full-time investor when I was always just one roof replacement, trashed unit, or lawsuit away from insolvency. While everyone thinks that landlords make tons of money, I sure didn't. The bank, the county, the contractors, and the attorneys all got paid before I did, and there was very little left over each month for me to reliably count on.

Expenses went up every year, and because of the stiff competition locking area rent rates in place, there was no way to recoup those higher costs. A single major setback (which I discovered over time was pretty much guaranteed) could blow up my entire cash flow for that year and sometimes even the next.

The National Apartment Association's research supports what a low-margin business rental housing is. According to their 2019 findings, each dollar in rent received is broken down the following ways[5]:

$0.39	Mortgage payment
$0.10	Capital expenditures
$0.27	Maintenance, utilities, insurance
$0.14	Property taxes
$0.09	**Profit**

Figure 1

I remember sharing the details of my business with a financial analyst who was interested in real estate investing. He asked me if I could quit my teaching job and rely on my properties for income. My lack of an answer made it crystal clear to both of us that it was time to accept the obvious: this was not the business I had been hoping for.

Looking back on those years as a real estate investor, the biggest and most expensive lesson I learned

---

[5]https://www.naahq.org/sites/default/files/naa-documents/dollarrent_v3.pdf

was **real estate investment wasn't worth the constant stress**. You can't put a dollar amount on being interrupted every holiday with a repair catastrophe or a furnace failure when you are trying to enjoy time with your family. I began feeling like I was on call twenty-four hours a day, providing high-quality housing to tenants, but receiving very little financial incentive in return.

None of the gurus that promoted real estate investment as the secret to financial independence ever addressed any of these issues, drawbacks, or the guaranteed burnout that comes with landlording. They were too busy convincing me how I would be a multimillionaire within ten years. It made me wonder if the gurus gained much more from the *promotion* of real estate investment rather than the actual *practice*.

There is no question that serious wealth is made in real estate. However, based on my own experiences, I wouldn't be surprised to learn that much of that wealth is skewed toward large investment companies rather than mom-and-pop organizations like mine. Either way, being a landlord or running a vacation rental is not going to be a good fit for every investor, which is why we need to consider a new way of making money in real estate—a way that's truly passive and truly profitable.

I will be exploring my experiences in real estate investment more fully in an upcoming book.

Recovery through Mortgage Loan Investing

Needless to say, after more than a decade, I realized real estate investing and landlording weren't going to get me the financial success and independence I wanted. Still, I thought that real estate might hold the key to realizing my future goals, but how?

I discovered the answer to this question in 2016, during a chance meeting at a real estate conference. An investor I met had transitioned out of rental investing and into mortgage loan investing. His story, which was very similar to mine, blew my mind. The difference was that as a mortgage loan investor, he ran a profitable, low-stress business from anywhere in the world. Payment collection and borrower communication were handled by a third-party loan servicer. Best of all, he was able to invest in loans secured by real estate without the myriad risks and complications that came with owning the property. It sounded too good to be true—but in this case, it wasn't.

Soon after I began purchasing mortgage loans as investments, I started selling my rental units, most of them at a loss from what I paid a decade earlier. I was so glad to walk away from the stress and headaches, I was willing to accept the loss.

With mortgage loan investing, I found I was better able to expand and grow in diverse markets across the country, without having to spend my weekends inspecting rentals and paying contractors, without the worry of flooded basements during every heavy rainstorm. Mortgage loan investing gave me a manageable way to enjoy the inflation resistance of real estate while ensuring I received regular distributions, rather than having appreciation locked up in equity. Even better, the distributions were ongoing, which meant I could live on or reinvest the income steadily, at the buying power of today's dollar.

As a real estate investor, I felt like I earned every dollar I ever made by dealing with stressful situations every day. This is not the case with mortgage loan investing, a truly passive method of secured lien holding with predictable payments. Part of the reason for this is that mortgage loans allow investors to leverage the traditional banking model—and if there's one thing banks are experts at, it's making money.

Considerations	Real Estate Investing	Loan Investing
Leverage	Purchase with only 30% down	Must pay cash
Appreciation	Appreciates over time	Depreciates as payments are made
Depreciation	Great tax benefits	No tax benefits
Transfer costs	$30,000 or more	Approximately $100
Headache factor	Tenants are difficult, demanding	No contact with borrowers
Capital expenditures	Frequently costly repairs	Not the lender's responsibility
Vacancy	Repairs, loss of rents	Paid in full when borrower sells home
Legal	Laws favor tenants	Laws protect lenders
Market diversification	Usually a single market	Nationwide
Liability	High risk, requires expensive insurance	Own the lien, not the property
Management	Requires staff, contractors	Can passively manage thousands of loans
Emotional equity	Tenants move for cheaper rent	Homeowners emotionally tied to homes
Financial sophistication	Tenants living paycheck to paycheck	Homeowners more financially sound
Wear and tear	Tenants hard on properties	Homeowners protect their #1 investment

Figure 2

Leveraging the Traditional Banking Model

In a post-Great Recession world, banks are leaders in safe lending. With the introduction of the Dodd–Frank Act, financial institutions have stiff regulatory compliance standards to maintain and rigorous capitalization requirements.[6] In short, banks that survived the financial crisis are stronger than they've ever been and new regulations, no matter how begrudgingly followed, are keeping them there.

Of the major changes the Dodd–Frank Act introduced to banks, two of the most interesting are the stricter requirements for mortgage lending and better safeguards for banks that follow them. One such change is found in the eight underwriting factors lenders are asked to consider when determining a borrower's ability to repay.[7] Another is found in the legal protection offered to lenders who keep borrower loan payments from going above 43 percent of their income.[8]

Sounds good for banks, right? But what about for investors? Well, if you're investing in mortgage loans that have been originated by banks under these stringent guidelines, it results in an inherent risk mitigation that might not exist with other investments.

---

[6]https://www.bankrate.com/banking/banks-safe-healthier-now-coronavirus-shock/
[7]https://www.federalregister.gov/documents/2013/01/30/2013-00736/ability-to-repay-and-qualified-mortgage-standards-under-the-truth-in-lending-act-regulation-z
[8]https://www.consumerfinance.gov/about-us/newsroom/consumer-financial-protection-bureau-issues-rule-to-protect-consumers-from-irresponsible-mortgage-lending/

It's not just newly originated loans that have risk-adjusted benefits for investors. Even loans originated before the 2008 Great Recession can have tremendous value with limited risk. Because these loans were issued to borrowers who kept up their payments, even while underwater during the financial crisis, most of them have already regained the equity lost during that stressful time. But beyond safety, mortgage loan investing offers an opportunity for alternative investors to find high profits—similar to those that banks secure for themselves. How? By taking advantage of the spread and amortization intrinsic to the traditional banking model.

Traditional Banking: The Net Interest Spread

When I talk about traditional banking, I'm referring to depository institutions, such as commercial banks, savings and loans, and credit unions. These are "banks" in the traditional sense; they accept deposits from borrowers and part of their business is lending out their depositors' funds to borrowers in the form of mortgage loans. In the next chapter, I'll talk more about other types of mortgage lenders.

The traditional banking model is surprisingly simple. In its most basic sense, it works like this:

ABC Credit Union accepts deposits from customers, paying interest of 2 percent on their deposits.

These deposits are pooled and funds are used to originate a mortgage loan to Joe Customer at 8 percent.

The bank requires a 20 percent down payment from Joe Customer, allowing them to finance 80 percent of the home's value.

The credit union's net interest spread is roughly 6 percent, which is the difference between what they receive in interest on home loans and their cost of funds, or what they pay in interest to their deposit customers.

Banks are in the business of money. Loaning it, securing it, and earning it. This is clearly seen from the simplicity and net interest spread built into the traditional banking model. While these factors lay the foundation for why mortgage loan investing can be low risk and profitable, there's a lot more to it than that.

Traditional Banking: Fees and Amortization

Another way that banks profit in mortgage lending is through the fees involved in originating a mortgage loan. If financial institutions can keep recycling their capital and charging borrowers fees that total 3 percent of each mortgage loan amount, it would make more sense to sell loans as quickly as possible.

If a financial institution originates only $20 million in loans per year and makes 3 percent of that total just in fees, that equals $600,000 profit per year! When you further consider that home buyers routinely finance their closing costs as part of the overall mortgage, the profits grow exponentially.

Banks also profit on lending through amortization. If you've ever taken out a home loan, you have seen the required Truth in Lending disclosure in Figure 3. Did you get sick to your stomach when you saw that making each minimum required payment over the life of the loan would drive up the total amount paid back on your loan *almost three times what you originally borrowed?*

Consider the following example for a $50,000 loan at 8 percent over thirty years:

ANNUAL PERCENTAGE RATE	FINANCE CHARGE	Amount Financed	Total of Payments
The cost of your credit as a yearly rate.	The dollar amount the credit will cost you.	The amount of credit provided to you or on your behalf.	The amount you will have paid after you have made all payments as scheduled.
8.000%	$82,076.80	$50,000.00	$132,076.80

Figure 3

You might think that this means a bank would want to hang on to your loan as long as possible to get all of that 300 percent markup, but thanks to amortization, which requires the largest percentage of interest at the beginning of the loan, banks don't need to. Because in addition to earning money from the spread we talked about in the last section, banks are earning most of the interest on your loan up front, in the first several years of payments.

Take a look at the amortization schedule for the loan discussed in Figure 3:

LIENLORD

Payment #	Date	Payment	Principal	Interest	Balance
1	Aug 12 2020	$366.88	$33.55	$333.33	$49,966.45
2	Sep 12 2020	$366.88	$33.77	$333.11	$49,932.68
3	Oct 12 2020	$366.88	$34.00	$332.88	$49,898.68
4	Nov 12 2020	$366.88	$34.22	$332.66	$49,864.46
5	Dec 12 2020	$366.88	$34.45	$332.43	$49,830.01
Year 1	2020	$1,834.40	$169.99	$1,664.41	$49,830.01
6	Jan 12 2021	$366.88	$34.68	$332.20	$49,795.33
7	Feb 12 2021	$366.88	$34.91	$331.97	$49,760.42
8	Mar 12 2021	$366.88	$35.14	$331.74	$49,725.28
9	Apr 12 2021	$366.88	$35.38	$331.50	$49,689.90
10	May 12 2021	$366.88	$35.61	$331.27	$49,654.29
11	Jun 12 2021	$366.88	$35.85	$331.03	$49,618.44
12	Jul 12 2021	$366.88	$36.09	$330.79	$49,582.35

Figure 4

The first monthly payment of $366.88 only applies $33.55 to principal. In fact, one year in, at your twelfth payment, you're still only paying $36.09 toward that principal balance—for a total of $417.65 paid toward your principal. In a YEAR! During that same time, you've paid $3,984.91 in interest. And that's only for *one loan!* Multiply that by a thousand loans, and you can see what money machines banks are.

Finally, banks cannot just continue to lend endlessly. They are bound by reserve ratios, or the amount they are required to keep liquid. If a bank is approaching their lending limits, but still wants to originate loans, it may decide to sell some of their older loans, or least desirable loans, in pools in order to create liquidity and continue lending and collecting origination fees.

And that's where you come in.

LIENLORD

Profiting with Mortgage Loans

While both banks and mortgage loan investors own loans and count on monthly loan income for profits, the mortgage loan investing business model differs from the bank's in one key way: investors don't need to originate mortgage loans. They don't need to evaluate debt-to-income ratios, collect required disclosures, or deal with compliance.

Instead, investors purchase loans that banks have already underwritten and approved. They do this in what's called the *secondary market*. And that's critical to how mortgage loan investors make money.

Loan Origination and the Secondary Market

When a person first buys a home, refinances a home, or gets an equity loan from a lender, it's a transaction within the primary mortgage market. Sometimes, lenders in the primary market want to sell off the loans they've originated or are servicing. One way to do this is by offering the loans for sale in the secondary mortgage market.

Think of it in the same way you would traditional public equity purchases. If an initial public offering (IPO) is a primary market offering, after that, stock purchases and sales take place in the secondary market.

Mortgage banks and nonbank lenders, which do not engage in the business of retail banking by accepting deposits from borrowers, originate mortgage loans from huge lines of credit, and immediately sell the loans on the secondary market, mainly to the government-sponsored enterprises (GSE) Fannie Mae and Freddie Mac. These loans, which have strict and extensive underwriting guidelines, are frequently packaged into securities, sold as bonds, guaranteed by the GSEs, and backed by the US Treasury. While these bonds are very safe investments, their yields are usually quite low—barely above US treasuries—and may not even beat inflation.

Depository institutions, a.k.a. traditional banks, are not in the business of creating securities from their mortgage holdings. Instead, they sell their loans in pools on the secondary market to recapitalize.

Entire loans sold in the secondary market are referred to as *whole loans*, because the bank sells the rights to the entire loan, not just a securitized piece of a loan pool.

There are many risk-reducing benefits to investing in whole loans through the secondary market, but one of the most important is that you can select loans on which borrowers have been making consistent payments.

Banks take something of a leap of faith when they originate a mortgage, especially with low down-payment loan programs. Will the borrower pay? When you invest in mortgage loans through the secondary market, you are able to review extremely detailed information about the pay history, with a tracking of payment dates, amounts, and late fees, sometimes going back for years. From that information, investors can select loans that have an established, on-time pay history.

Investing in financial institution–generated secondary mortgage market loans means gaining an inherent stability and security because investors know that

- loan documents and procedures adhere to all applicable state and federal lending guidelines and servicing histories and data are accurate;
- there is usually no need to interior appraise or visit the property;
- loan servicers collect any payments and keep track of tax records;
- the payment terms cannot be changed unless the lender consents;
- borrowers are required to continue making payments and maintain insurance to retain their property. This is important because history shows that even in times of economic hardship, borrowers protect their homes. According to the Federal Reserve, foreclosure rates on residential mortgage loans during the financial crisis of 2008 to 2013 never exceeded 11.54 percent.[9] The truth is, Americans have, on average, more wealth in their homes than in their savings and retirement accounts combined.[10] Most Americans' greatest source of wealth is the equity in their homes.

---

[9]https://www.federalreserve.gov/releases/chargeoff/delallsa.htm
[10]https://www.federalreserve.gov/publications/files/scf17.pdf

According to Black Knight, the average homeowner with a mortgage has $113,900 of equity in their home.[11] That's a powerful motivator, but besides the financial equity, they also have emotional equity. What's the likelihood a homeowner will pack up and leave a home they have equity in and that they have invested their time and money into upgrading? In my experience, it virtually never happens. Borrowers fight to keep their homes, which is what mortgage loan investors want; and

- mortgage loan investors don't own the property, just the *lien* on the property. I spent thirteen years as a real estate investor, an experience that taught me that owning and managing property as an investment is a high-risk, high-stress responsibility to be avoided. As a mortgage loan investor, the collateral pledged as security for the primary loan secures your investment. To the homeowner, the underlying collateral is more than just a means to mitigating investment risk; it's the homeowner's prized possession. It's their biggest investment, and the place where they keep their families happy and safe. It's also up to them to maintain and repair it. For an investor, this can be the best of both worlds. You don't own the property, but you have the right to foreclose and sell the property at auction to recoup your investment if the borrower defaults.

---

[11]https://investor.blackknightinc.com/investors/press-releases/press-release-details/2018/Black-Knights-Mortgage-Monitor-Despite-Record-Setting-Tappable-Equity-Growth-Share-of-Total-Equity-Withdrawn-Hits-Four-Year-Low-in-Q1-2018/default.aspx

Your Investment, Your Choice

When banks are in the business of lending, they have certain guidelines they need to follow to ensure they are meeting the investment needs of the communities they serve. The Community Reinvestment Act (CRA) requires banks to lend to a variety of different borrowers for a multitude of property types throughout their community.

Mortgage loan investors reviewing offerings on the secondary market for opportunities are not held to the same standards. We have the power to choose the types of properties and markets we invest in. This offers a level of diversification that can go far in further reducing risk and improving returns.

One of the most powerful advantages of mortgage loan investing is geographic diversification, or the ability to purchase loans in multiple markets in multiple states. Real estate investors tend to purchase properties only in one local market, which can expose an investor to tremendous risk during natural disasters or economic recessions. Since not all markets will be affected the same way during recessions, the ability to create geographic diversification further reduces portfolio risk.

In addition, thanks to this level of flexibility, investors can choose to only invest in loans secured by owner-occupied homes in the markets they choose. Investors can even choose collateral properties that show a clear pride of ownership and are located in low-crime neighborhoods.

Mortgage loan investing is a very passive, scalable, diversifiable, low-stress business. In mortgage investing, all the major responsibilities are outsourced to experts. My main responsibilities as an investor are

- finding new sellers of loans that meet my criteria; and
- reviewing loans for purchase.

I even outsource my bookkeeping and accounting responsibilities. But there's more to the reasoning that the simplistic model makes mortgage loans the gold standard of alternative investments. There is the financial component. In other words, it comes down to yield.

Securing Your Yield

An investor's annual return over the life of an investment is called *yield to maturity,* or just *yield.* I always purchase on yield, and I firmly believe that buying on yield, based on the individual risk assessment of each loan, is the wisest strategy.

There's a common misconception that yield and return on investment (ROI) are the same measurement. They are not. ROI is a measure of an investment's return relative to its cost. To calculate the ROI of an investment, one simply divides the net profit by the amount of the investment. ROI is more appropriately used once an investment is exited.

Yield, on the other hand, represents the ongoing future income on an investment. Yield includes the element of duration and is better used for measuring future investment returns.

Rate of return (ROR) is another factor that often gets confused with yield. As with ROI, ROR will depend on the total amount earned over the life of the investment, versus the asset's cost and accounting for inflation.

Calculating Yield

Calculating yield is quite simple, but requires a financial calculator. The financial calculator I use is called 10bii, and I have it on my smartphone. For the purposes of basic yield and pricing calculations, I only use four keys at the top of the 10bii calculator:

N	I/YR	PV	PMT

N: number of payments remaining
I/YR: interest per year, or yield
PV: present value (purchase price, entered as a negative number)
PMT: monthly payment

Here's an example of a simple yield calculation to help you understand the process. Let's say you were reviewing a loan that had the following characteristics:

- 132 payments (11 years) remaining
- 8 percent note interest rate
- $43,285.21 unpaid principal balance (UPB/PV)
- $494.12 monthly payment

If you pay a flat $43,285.21 for the loan, your yield, or future ongoing income on the investment, would be 8 percent. Few would argue that an 8 percent yield is too low, but what if you wanted more? What if you wanted a yield of 12 percent each year over the remaining eleven years of the loan? This can be accomplished by reducing the amount that you pay for the loan. Using a financial

LIENLORD

calculator, you would solve for the desired purchase price at a 12 percent yield by entering the following data:

N: number of payments	I/YR: desired yield	PV: purchase price	PMT: monthly payment
132	12	Unknown	494.12

Figure 5

By entering the data and then pressing the PV key, you will get an answer of -36,125.48. PV is expressed as a negative, because this is what you are paying; it is money out of pocket. Therefore, our simple yield calculation returned that we should offer the seller of the loan $36,125.48.

By reducing our purchase price to $7,159.73 less than the total amount owed by the borrower, we pay a discounted price for the loan and drive up the yield so it exceeds the interest rate of the loan. Therefore, the purchase price must be discounted for us to achieve our desired yield. This brings up the important term of *par*, something you might have heard if you've traded bonds.

When a bond is sold at par, it means the sale price is equal to the bond's face value. When mortgage loans sell at par, it means they sell for 100 percent of the UPB. In the initial example, a loan selling at par would be selling for the full $43,285.21.

I decide my minimum yield when I purchase a loan. By calculating the monthly payment, the number of payments remaining on a loan, and the purchase price, I can determine exactly how much I will make each year over the life of the loan. Since I am buying the full unpaid principal balance (UPB) at a discount, if the loan is paid off early (most are), my yield will increase even more. And if I decide to sell the loan, I can sell the remaining payments to another investor.

This, however, is where that balance I mentioned earlier between yield and risk comes in. Because the messier the characteristics of a loan are, the greater it will be discounted. If the borrower has missed or been late on a couple of payments since origination, or the owner of the loan is missing a loan document, or when the borrower has just filed a bankruptcy, it introduces additional risk (most of the time negligible) into the scenario and, as a result, increases the discount and the yield.

Ultimately, potential yield means nothing if you never collect any money. I would rather have a lower, yet still competitive yield and on-time payments than a huge potential yield that I never collect on. Remember, lending is based on risk. We can mitigate this risk with our lien, but we want to choose deals that keep us in the payment business, not those that push us into the litigation and eviction business.

Not all loans sold at a discount are high risk, however. Why would a seller of a perfectly low-risk mortgage loan accept less than the full amount owed for a loan? Because of the time value of money.

Time Value of Money

Due to its earning potential, one dollar today is worth more than the same dollar will be in ten or twenty years—because today that dollar can be invested and compounded in value year after year. Factor in inflation, and the future value of one dollar drops even more.

When banks originate a mortgage loan, they have two choices. They can wait a maximum of thirty years to receive the last payment and get all their money back at a future value with cash that's worth less than it would be today, or they can sell the loan to another investor during the first few years of the loan and capitalize on the fees they charge on newly originated and amortized loans.

Inflation alone causes the value of every mortgage payment to drop. That $494.12 payment? Today, during year one, it's worth a lot more money than it will be by year twenty after inflation drags down the spending power of each dollar. For banks, mortgages are depreciating assets.[12] If they hold these assets for the full thirty years, they will likely be worth significantly less than they are today.

And remember that amortization example we looked at before? Banks can only originate those thousands of loans when they have the available capital to do so. Divesting some older mortgage assets means freeing up capital today and putting the time value of money back on their side.

Let's look at an example of a discounted mortgage loan purchase to understand why a bank would agree to sell at discount.

Loan amount	$50,000
Borrower's interest rate	8%
Monthly payment	$366.88
Amortization	30 years

Figure 6

---

[12]https://www.econlib.org/archives/2003/09/mortgage_deprec.html

After five years of consistent payments, the bank decides to sell this loan as part of a pool to an investment fund needing to earn 11 percent on its money.

Original loan amount	-$50,000
Origination fees	+$2,500
Principal and interest collected over 5 years	+$22,012.80
Discounted sale of loan	+$37,432.42
Bank profit after five years	**$11,945.22**

Figure 7

Keep in mind that the profit in Figure 7 does not include the yield spread for the bank's cost of capital. When we take that into consideration, their profit is much higher. Selling this loan allows the bank to make more in fees by originating a new loan, constantly recycling their capital.

Selling mortgage loans at a discount allows banks to avoid the deleterious effects of inflation and lost earning potential. It makes mortgage loans more attractive to investors and much more liquid for banks.

Investor versus Bank

If it's in a bank's best interests to sell some mortgage loans, you might be wondering why it's in an investor's best interest to buy them. After all, don't you have to worry about the time value of money too?

First, you have to consider the benefits of mortgage loan investing against that of other forms of investment you can make. Whereas a bank has that potential to originate thousands of loans when they have the available capital, retail investors like us might not have the same financial wherewithal. Further, because most of us don't want to spend our investment principal, we are happy to receive monthly cash flows that provide us with a combination of return of our principal, along with interest income at a predetermined minimum yield.

Investors are generally focused on yield for the part of their portfolio they allocate to mortgage loan investing. Mortgage loan yields are generally much higher than bonds. It's not unusual to see yields of 8 to 10 percent on mortgage loans, which is really hard to do with bonds or annuities. And unlike annuities, the mortgage loan's payments don't stop when an investor passes away.

Investors are also in a more favorable position than banks in terms of capital outlay. When a bank originates a mortgage, it lends 100 percent of the loan balance, and is limited to the interest rate on the note. Mortgage loan investors purchase loans at 50 to 90 percent of what is owed, which means if the loan is paid off early, our yield will *dramatically* increase.

Investor versus Bank, Part 2

We've focused a lot on yield in this chapter, but there is actually another way investors can profit in mortgage loan investment, and that occurs when they've purchased a loan at a discount and that loan is paid off early.

While yield calculations assume all payments are made to maturity, purchasing loans at a discount can create a huge ROI gain if a loan is paid off early, and they usually are. *The average mortgage loan is paid off within ten years.*[13]

Consider the following example on a second lien loan I just purchased in California:

Purchase price (for investor)	$21,000.00
UPB (unpaid principal balance)	$27,376.22
Borrower's interest rate	6.99%
Monthly payment	$351.84
Payments remaining	104
My investment yield	14.18%
Total collected over life of loan	$36,591.36

Figure 8

If this loan is paid off after twelve months, the investor would receive a total of $29,216.96 on a loan they paid just $21,000 to own.

12 monthly payments of $351.84= $4,222.08
Payoff balance after 12 payments at 6.99% interest= $24,994.88

$4,222.08 + 24,994.88= $29,216.96

---

[13]https://www.colliers.com/-/media/697C933563184B1183435095CAB54459.ashx

This would result in realizing an additional 19 percent ROI, not including the twelve payments received before the early payoff. If we include the $4,222.08 in payments received over the twelve months, our total yield due to the early payoff is 39 percent! The investor could then take the $24,994.88 payoff and purchase another loan, or possibly two! It doesn't take very long for income to compound in mortgage loan investment.

While this section may seem complicated, the basic point here is that buying a mortgage loan as an investment is like buying a neat, packaged set of payments. It's highly defined and measurable, and far fewer variables occur than in traditional real estate investing.

The loan you may be considering buying might not be the only lien on the underlying house. A property's *first lien* is the loan secured earliest, which has the priority repayment position in the event of a sale or refinance. The *second lien* is the next loan secured after the first lien and has second priority for repayment.

Don't let this discussion overwhelm you. When we calculate yield for our investment purposes, we are not concerned about what percentage of each payment is principal versus interest. Our yield calculations are based simply on the number of payments and the amount of each payment required, which makes our lives and investments that much easier.

If borrowers pay extra each month, that's great for us; our loan will be paid back even quicker than we originally calculated, and our yield will increase even higher than we originally expected. The only downside to an early payoff? We will have to go back out to market and find a replacement loan, but chances are the replacement loan will have a higher monthly payment and a higher UPB. If not, we can likely buy two loans! Think about how quickly this strategy can multiply, and you're starting to understand the benefits of mortgage loan investing.

Now that we are on the topic of doubling our investment portfolios, let's examine how compounding interest can double an investment portfolio.

Compounding and the Rule of 72

If you are starting to get excited about investing in mortgage loans because of their simplicity and profitability, hold on to your hat, because it gets better.

Every month that you receive payments from borrowers, you have the opportunity to reinvest those funds. And when the homeowners pay off the loan early, those funds get reinvested, too, often back into a new loan. Thanks to the Rule of 72, you can figure out at what interest rate you need to reinvest those funds to double them during the timeline you choose.

The Rule of 72 is a mathematical formula that allows you to estimate the time it will take money to double at various investment rates. In general, you can expect money invested with a 1 percent return to double in seventy-two years. A 2 percent return doubles money in about thirty-six years. A 3 percent return doubles money in about twenty-four years, and so on.

If you earned 9 percent annually on your portfolio, it would take you eight years of compounding interest before your portfolio doubled in value. The formula for the Rule of 72 is:

((72/interest rate) = number of years to double)

The key for mortgage loan investors who aren't using their returns for current income is to continue reinvesting the earnings, keeping in mind that consistency over time beats a couple of great years over the long run—something I illustrate more in the Stocks section.

Too often, I hear from people who keep their funds sitting in their IRA account because they're waiting for an astronomical investment return. What these folks don't understand is that, thanks to inflation, money not invested decreases in value each month, and accurate portfolio performance measurements must average in the amount of time investment funds went undeployed.

I am a firm believer that returns are based on risk. Be very cautious of any offering that touts both double-digit returns and low risk. These types of offerings could end up costing you your entire investment.

Slow and steady growth wins the race. It's much better to keep your money working for you consistently over time than it is to have it sitting on the sidelines decreasing in value, hoping that some "home run" investment comes along. Few of us would be shocked with a 9 percent return, but when you consider that it can double your money in eight years, it certainly sounds better than leaving those funds doing nothing in your IRA or risking their loss with that "sure thing" investment.

Downsides of Mortgage Loan Investing (Or Are They?)

Every investment has risks, limitations, and drawbacks that impact its appropriate level of asset allocation in each investor's portfolio. It's important to learn about these potential downsides for a couple reasons.

First, doing so helps you determine the appropriate weight for that investment within your portfolio. Second, learning about the downsides can sometimes give you an insight into ways they become upsides.

Full Cost Up Front

Real estate investors regularly rely on leverage to build their portfolio. Purchasing properties with just 20 to 30 percent down through commercial loans is the goal, allowing a bank to finance the rest.

As I've mentioned, mortgage loan investors, on the other hand, pay the full amount the loan is being sold for.

There is no leverage in mortgage loan investment, meaning banks will not finance mortgage loans. This can mean that an investor's funds don't go as far—if an investor has $100,000 to invest, they might be able to buy four $100,000 rental homes, but only four $25,000 mortgage loans.

Leverage sounds like a pretty big advantage given to real estate investors, but it can get risky. In every loan transaction, the lender puts themselves in the best position to secure their capital. In other words, they will set themselves up to collect their money whether you can afford to keep paying or not. Banks require most investors to personally guarantee commercial loans, which means that if the borrower defaults, the lender can make a claim against the borrower's, or in this case, investor's personal assets.

Let's say that after you buy a multi-unit building with bank financing, there is a severe economic downturn. Your tenants can't afford to pay their rent because they are out of work. You're collecting only 50 percent of the monthly income you expected and, frankly, depend on, and you're unable to continue to meet the large mortgage payment and pay for repairs, insurance, utilities, and real estate taxes. You have burned through your cash reserves trying to keep the building afloat and now have to come up with extensive legal fees in order to evict tenants who cannot pay rent.

After a long eviction, you are faced with staggering expenses to rehab the units to get them ready to re-rent. Do you expect the bank to cut you some slack and allow you to not make loan payments for twenty-four months while you try to get back on your feet? Or how about asking them to loan you more money to pay the legal fees, fix up the units, and re-rent them? You might hope that, but they won't do it.

Eventually, the lender will file foreclosure and seek a deficiency judgment against you personally, which would allow them to recover the amount you owe the bank from any personal assets you own. At this point, to save your personal assets, you will have few options other than filing bankruptcy.

In my experience, most real estate investors vastly overleverage and don't maintain the massive reserves needed to survive an economic downturn. They want to put their cash to work as quickly as possible by purchasing more units. Unfortunately, too many real estate investors are financially destroyed during downturns and lose not only their credit, but also all the cash down payments they invested as well.

It's just too risky for my appetite, and instead of holding on to huge cash reserves to offset the risks in real estate, I would rather place those in an investment that returns less volatile income.

This accelerated risk for real estate investors taking advantage of leverage is, in actuality, a downside. It means that mortgage loan investment's lack of leverage is a benefit for the investor. Since we have paid cash for a loan, we know our maximum downside risk: the price of the loan. We needn't worry about considerable additional expenses piling up on us when we can't afford to pay them, or having those expenses jeopardize our ability to maintain ownership of our assets.

Appreciation

The biggest advantage to real estate ownership is appreciation. Because real estate investors own their properties, they participate in the growth of its value. They can realize the profits from this growth by selling the property for a higher price than they purchased it for or by pulling cash out through loans. How significant an advantage is this?

Well, between 1969 and 2016, the average appreciation rate was 5.4 percent.[14] During the eleven-year period of January 2009 and January 2019, the average home price appreciated more than 50 percent.[15]

The problem with counting on appreciation, besides the fact that you don't know the property will have appreciated by the time you want to sell it (just ask investors who retired and wanted to sell property in 2009), is that leverage makes potential appreciation look way better on paper than it is in real life.

Let's look at an example. An investor purchases a six-unit building for $500,000, making a 25 percent down payment of $125,000. Leverage allows the investor to count on the $500,000 purchase price as the basis for the asset's appreciation, not just their down payment.

If that $500,000 building appreciates at 3 percent per year, then in ten years, it should be worth $650,000. Because the investor has only invested 25 percent of the purchase price as the down payment, in theory the asset can produce a cash-on-cash return of over 100 percent ($125,000 costs, $150,000 profit).

On paper, it seems like a no-brainer, right? Especially when you compare it to a similar mortgage loan investment, which has a cash-on-cash return of 10 percent.

---

[14]https://escholarship.org/content/qt31q9h8m0/qt31q9h8m0.pdf
[15]https://fred.stlouisfed.org/series/MSPUS

But wait—not so fast. This example doesn't take into consideration any of the following potential losses absorbed by the investor:

- large capital expenditures
- routine maintenance/repairs
- pest control
- vacancies
- unit rehab between tenants
- overcharging contractors/property managers
- evictions
- lawsuits
- fires/floods/natural disasters
- increasing costs for property taxes
- Increasing costs for hazard, liability, and umbrella insurance
- utilities
- increasing competition flattening rent increases
- city fines/inspections
- break-ins
- closing costs
- Agent/property management fees

All these expenses can massively derail profits during that ten-year period, offsetting any appreciation. They drive down the net gain and impact the investor's liquidity along the way.

Let's face it—owning property comes with huge liability risks. In order to profit, most landlords are forced to manage their properties at a substandard level, which devalues the property over time and increases the risk of lawsuits. Speaking of which, the amount of insurance landlords require is staggering. From hazard to liability to umbrella to workers' compensation, it's not just about protecting the property but also tenants, guests, and workers.

In a very serious event, such as a fire, there is a high likelihood the owner's coverage won't be enough to pay out the totality of claims. Since most investors underinsure to maximize profits, they face the risk of attorneys going after their personal possessions and accounts, which a simple LLC won't prevent.

What if a tenant brings something onto the property—a pit bull or a trampoline, for instance—and someone is seriously injured? Who is the attorney going to recoup damages from? The tenant? Or the property owner? Even if the owner didn't know about the dog or the trampoline and didn't give the tenant permission to have them, the owner is still liable for the damages.

Or, what if the handyman the landlord uses frequently for repairs gets hurt while working on the property? An investor may think the handyman is an independent contractor, but a judge will likely rule under workers' compensation laws that the property owner is responsible for the injuries and/or disability.

And, as I briefly mentioned, none of this considers the risk that the property will lose value either because of mismanagement, vacancy, neighborhood, or economic factors. Remember, only investors purchase commercial buildings, not homeowners, so the purchasers don't fall in love with room sizes or colors or appliances. They only fall in love with the numbers and cap rate, and only buy when they can get a deal. It's no secret that tenants are hard on rentals, and owners must project very generously for ongoing building repairs.

Furthermore, not all properties appreciate equally. I held single-family rentals for over ten years that actually depreciated in value from what I invested into them, between acquisition and rehab costs.

Many investors choose lower-value (under $150,000), single-family rentals because of the cash flow and perceived stability, like I did. Yet, in my experience, these are speculative investments, mainly driven by investor demand during real estate market upswings. Unfortunately, markets with numerous single-family rentals are considered less desirable, tend not to be well maintained by the investor owners, and attract fewer homeowners.

I have also watched investors move into markets betting on gentrification, only to see those markets drop in value during market corrections. In some cases, the investors have trusted city- or county-wide plans for improvement that seemed to be pointing the area in one economic direction, only to see plans change, funding fall through, and improvement projects scrapped.

Leverage is helpful to real estate investors who want to grow a portfolio quickly, but it still takes time to make a portfolio of rental buildings appreciate. During this time, investors are exposed to a multitude of risks that just grow, which for me, at least, begs the question: *Is it worth it?*

For mortgage loan investors, however, the value of the loans we purchase slowly decrease over time as we collect payments and the loan is paid back, because there is no underlying physical asset.

This definitely represents a difference compared to real estate investing, but remember that we determined our minimum yield when we purchased the loan. Since loans are usually paid off prior to the maturity date and we purchased at a discount, we will get a nice additional return on our investment when that happens.

In addition, rather than pay interest on a loan to extract value out of a property, like a real estate investor must do if they don't want to sell, we get capital back every month that we can continue to reinvest, allowing us to increase our cash flow dramatically over time.

While we all like to focus on the appreciation of real estate, which is certainly a benefit for real estate investors, it's also important to consider that there is a real risk of values dropping during a recession. That is a risk real estate investors are exposed to, but mortgage loan investors are not. During the 2008 recession, home prices fell 33 percent.[16] In 2020, we're seeing real estate values falling in some markets due to the financial pressures brought on by the pandemic. And, as I'll discuss in the Weighing Traditional Investments against Mortgage Loans chapter, while economic downturns almost certainly contribute to falling home values, they do not necessarily trigger high rates of foreclosure, which is good news for mortgage loan investors.

Personally, I would much rather buy a set number of payments from a mortgage loan and not have the responsibilities and headaches of property ownership, even if I miss out on the potential property appreciation. While appreciation is nice—when it happens—it usually requires a decade or more, and for investors with rental properties, it's always offset by large capital expenditure requirements.

I hear stories of investors buying rental properties with cash flows of only $100 after fixed monthly expenses. I shudder when I hear that because I can guarantee that

---

[16]https://www.washingtonpost.com/news/business/wp/2018/10/04/feature/10-years-later-how-the-housing-market-has-changed-since-the-crash/

person they will lose money over time due to all the variables involved with real estate investment. Whether it's a new roof, foundation, concrete, porches, sewer, plumbing, electrical, HVAC, tuckpointing, siding, and/or windows, you can always count on properties breaking down, ultimately offsetting gains in appreciation.

For me, going into an investment knowing exactly what I'm buying, what I'm getting, and what my expenses will be has proven to be a much faster route to financial freedom than dealing with tenants, toilets, termites, and trash.

Depreciation and Tax Benefits

Taxes are a consideration for every investor. Real estate investors, in particular, have some tax advantages that those of us investing in mortgage loans do not get. Like many things, however, these advantages do have a darker side.

One of the most notable tax benefits enjoyed by real estate investors is depreciation. Certain investors, including those with rental property, can write off the loss of value that comes from wear and tear since this use depreciates the property over the years. Depreciation adds a great tax benefit to the bottom-line income of real estate investors, but there is a hitch.

The fact that depreciation is a write-off shows that the IRS knows rental properties break down quickly and require consistent, expensive repairs. That's why the tax code gives such generous depreciation allowances, allowing investors to depreciate the building over a twenty-seven-and-a-half-year period (thirty-nine years for commercial properties). But that write-off ends even quicker when the property is sold. It's at that point that the depreciated value is considered "recaptured" and is then taxed as ordinary income, with a current cap of 25 percent.[17]

Real estate investments made with IRA accounts **cannot** be depreciated and have a long list of restrictions and potential taxations (including UBIT) that you should review carefully with your IRA custodian and CPA. You may find that investing in rental properties in an IRA can actually result in you paying *more* in taxes.

Another potential problem is that we don't know if and how these tax breaks will continue. Tax laws in the 1980s allowed for first-year depreciation of 11.7 percent. Today, first-year depreciation is capped at 3.63 percent. Who knows what the future brings for this and other aspects of real estate investment taxation?[18]

For these reasons, I am very comfortable guaranteeing you that taxes in the future will be higher than they are now, and the government may target tax breaks and incentives for real estate investors. If the tax breaks go away, what benefits will be left?

The problem with depreciation and loss is that for underwriting purposes, banks routinely only credit investors for 75 percent of their rental income. This helps them account for expenses related to vacancies and repairs. Unless an investor has huge cash flows or a huge W2 income, they run the risk of not being able to qualify for continued mortgages. In fact, the more units you have, the

---

[17]https://www.irs.gov/publications/p544#en_US_2019_publink1 00072564

[18]https://mf.freddiemac.com/docs/tcja-report.pdf

LIENLORD

more likely it will appear to banks that you are operating at a loss.
Other tax benefits given to real estate investors include:

- cost of repairs
- maintenance and upkeep expenses
- property taxes
- management fees
- legal fees
- advertising costs

Sure, a deduction for all these expenses is helpful, but consider the fact that real estate investors have to keep the capital on hand to pay for all those expenses, whenever and however often they arise, and you can see how quickly the downsides of real estate investing outweigh the tax advantages.

As a mortgage loan investor, all I own, literally, are two signed documents that give me the ability to collect a set number of payments, and the right to a residential property as collateral. It's well worth the trade-off because mortgage loan investing is a much more scalable business.

LIENLORD

Weighing Traditional Investments against Mortgage Loans

I want to make it clear that I'm not in favor of mortgage loans replacing traditional investments in an investor's portfolio. Every investor has a complicated combination of risk tolerance, time horizon, accumulation goals, net worth, and income needs. Therefore, every investor, with the help of a seasoned advisor, needs to find their own appropriate and effective asset mix.

My goal in this section is not to tout mortgage loan investing as a superior option to any other kind of investing, but to help the reader understand how mortgage loan investments stack up against more traditional investments. Doing this will allow more investors and their advisors to determine the appropriate place for mortgage loans in their portfolio.

I view mortgage loan investing playing a complementary role in a portfolio. These assets help improve diversification and are noncorrelated, meaning they are not affected by swings in the stock market. They add balance for many investors and a source of strong, predictable income for those who need it. But again, I want to stress that mortgage loans are just one component of a diversified, well-balanced portfolio.

Too many financial advisors are discouraged or even prevented from researching alternative investments such as mortgage loans or mortgage loan funds. The pool of what they offer clients is a tiny slice of the investable universe. It often consists only of Wall Street–related investments too volatile for a large stake of client assets and which often don't address the need for high-yield income generation.

The stigma that alternative investments are "too risky" to recommend makes little sense when you consider that stock investing success relies on a combination of consumer confidence, investor demand, and the willingness of corporations to act in their investors' best interests. Switch over to high-yield corporate bonds, and you have to rely on the company to make the coupon payments and pay back the principal, something studies show might not be as reliable as you've been told.

Let's take a closer look at some often-promoted investments to see how they stack up against mortgage loan investing. I'll kick it off with the big one—stocks.

Stocks

I was first introduced to stocks, which represent shares of ownership in an underlying company, when I was sixteen. My grandfather, who was retired during my entire youth, was an active stock market investor before the internet age. He introduced me to *Value Line*, an equity research company with a series of hard-bound research and ratings books at the library, very similar to a set of encyclopedias.[19] He taught me what to look for in stocks and how to integrate a stockbroker's advice. I still remember our experiments of picking stocks, pricing them out per share, and tracking our portfolios.

Trading stocks seemed, to me, overly complicated with no real assurance of success. The whole process seemed more like throwing darts at a board than it did controlled research resulting in successful returns. But my biggest problem with the market was that I didn't like the stress of having to accept losses.

Take a look at almost any generic asset allocation pie chart and you will see that stocks are pushed as the primary investment for most people during their younger, income-earning years. Why? Because conventional wisdom tells us that stocks grow. And grow. Did you know that if you invested $100 in Amazon back in 1997, it would be worth about $196,635 today?[20] If you invested $100 in Microsoft in 1986, it would be worth about $26,100. That same $100 in Apple in 1980? It would be worth about $106,391 today!

These numbers aren't untrue, but they are pretty optimistic. Because for every one Wall Street unicorn that's grown exponentially in forty years, there are thousands of companies that have gone bust. So, sure, $300 spread between Amazon, Microsoft, and Apple between 1980 and 1997 could have given you more than $300,000 today, but $300 in Enron, Compaq, and WorldCom might have given you losses or, worse, nothing at all.

---

[19]https://www.valueline.com/
[20]Yahoo! Finance. Prices accessed 8/30/2020.

The Problem of Picking Winners

There's no bright, blinking neon arrow flashing over the stocks that are going to grow over the years, and there's no specter of doom standing over those that will not. As of 2020, there were roughly 2,800 stocks listed on the New York Stock Exchange and 3,300 on the NASDAQ.[21,22] Which of the thousands are worth investing in? Probably not many. Just five stocks on the S&P 500, which lists 500 tech stocks, are pulling up the average of the whole index.[23] I don't know about you, but when it comes to being an individual investor trying to pick winners out of pools that big, I don't like my odds. And that inclination isn't just a feeling—it's backed by facts.

For fifty-five years, the Center for Research in Security Prices (CRSP) has maintained a database tracking historical security prices and returns.[24] Studies analyzing that database have found that between 1926 and 2016, the median length of time securities stayed listed was just seven-and-a-half years before disappearing into obscurity, taking investor cash with them.[25] That's overwhelming to think about, so let's go smaller and look at the S&P 500. Between 1980 and 2014, 320 listings had

---

[21] https://www.advfn.com/nyse/newyorkstockexchange.asp

[22] https://www.advfn.com/nasdaq/nasdaq.asp

[23] https://www.washingtonpost.com/business/2020/08/19/tech-stocks-markets/

[24] http://www.crsp.org/

[25] https://poseidon01.ssrn.com/delivery.php?ID=586024090004
10407708910301811911410503605306704506208709108908
41190130680850980821040330160120310480480130810850
17099088114018000904094009064094095018102026036012
09712710711110912012608609612706901508906702909006
70210650050081240850240250008&EXT=pdf

been removed from this list due to "business distress."[26] And according to J.P. Morgan, a steady stream of these companies faced their distress during times of economic expansion, not recession. The year this book was written, we saw massive volatility thanks to an election, a pandemic, and massive unemployment. Imagine trying to pick a winner with this level of volatility.[27]

All this should help you see that the odds are against you when you try to pick stocks, but I want to throw one research paper quote at you to help drive this point home. When researching whether stocks outperform treasury bills, researchers found that:

"... the best-performing 4% of listed companies explain the net gain for the entire US stock market since 1926, as other stocks collectively matched Treasury bills."
—"Do Stocks Outperform Treasury Bills?" Department of Finance, W. P. Carey School of Business, Arizona State University, May 2018

It doesn't take a virus, housing market collapse, or dotcom bubble burst to create losses for individual investors like you and me. Attempting to pick winning stocks is like betting against the house in Vegas. The odds are not in our favor, and most people are going to lose, most of the time. So much so that even highly trained,

---

[26]https://www.jpmorgan.com/cm/BlobServer/Eye_on_the_Market_September_2014_-_Executive_Summary.pdf
[27]https://www.forbes.com/sites/sergeiklebnikov/2020/09/30/stocks-close-a-dismal-september-as-investors-prepare-for-an-even-rockier-october/#50e1caf7e4b2

experienced financial professionals have a poor record of picking stocks that beat the market.[28]

Maybe It's All In the Timing

Another current stock investors fight against is timing. Let's look at a portfolio at the tail end of 1997 holding Microsoft, Bank of the Ozarks, and Mattel, all purchased from a broker, using a cell phone with a retractable antenna. But let's up the ante. Let's say the investor was fifty-five years old, just ten years away from retirement, and threw $100,000 into those positions. Now, we reach the year 2007, the cell phone has been replaced by a Blackberry, and our investor has a portfolio balance of $366,427 the day they retire.

Almost two years after retiring, in February 2009, just as our investor needed to start liquidating their portfolio to take some income distributions, the market crashed and the value of all their investments fell to $220,841.[29] Now, our investor has to liquidate a higher number of shares early on in their retirement just to get the amount they need for a distribution. This leaves fewer shares in their portfolio, which means less opportunity for recovery and growth when the market rebounds.

The above situation is an example of *sequence of returns risk*, and it causes lasting damage. Just as compounding interest and returns can drive accumulation, selling a large chunk of shares at a low price (or a loss) early in your retirement can devastate your ability to

---

[28]https://www.aei.org/carpe-diem/more-evidence-that-its-really-hard-to-beat-the-market-over-time-95-of-finance-professionals-cant-do-it/

[29]https://www.portfoliovisualizer.com/backtest-portfolio

maintain distributions and live out a comfortable retirement.

Time is touted as a great friend to the stock investor, when it can just as easily be the enemy. Proponents of stock market investing hold out 10 percent as a reasonable expectation for returns, a number that's often based on growth of an entire index during a historical period.[30] Please tell that to investors who lost their savings with WorldCom, Pets.com, Enron, and the thousands of delisted stocks removed from the NYSE over the years.

Stocks may have a place in your portfolio. That's for you and your advisor to determine. For my part, I am uncomfortable with the idea that hardworking Americans can have a large portion of their retirement savings wiped out during one major market correction, and it can take years to regain those losses—if they can at all.

While we *do* know where the market has been, we *don't* know where it's headed. Of the crashes that have occurred during my lifetime, the one thing they all had in common was that very few of us saw them coming. The stakes are too high to take chances when an investor's retirement is at risk.

Can we—or *should* we—expect an average 10 percent stock market return in the future? I don't know, but if there's any doubt, I would argue that investors should look at putting a small amount of their portfolio into alternative investments, such as mortgage loans, both to hedge against loss and to provide some steady income security.

---

[30]https://www.investopedia.com/ask/answers/042415/what-average-annual-return-sp-500.asp#:~:text=The%20S%26P%20500%20index%20is,since%20its%20inception%20through%202019.

Let's look at yet another not-so-nice gift that time brings to stock investors: volatility.

Volatility and Returns

Most people accept the volatility of the stock market as a natural, unavoidable part of investing. Some even embrace it, under the strategy of *dollar-cost averaging*. This strategy involves investing a specified amount periodically into a certain stock, ensuring that the investor buys both when the stock price is up and when it's down. Since the market is impossible to time, dollar-cost averaging ensures the investor buys both during highs and lows, thus averaging out their cost basis and better managing volatility.

Example: Dollar-Cost Averaging

	Q1	Q2	Q3	Q4	Avg price p/s
20 shares ABC	5.75 p/s	5.00 p/s	6.00 p/s	5.80 p/s	$5.64
80 shares ABC			6.00 p/s		$6.00

Figure 9

It might sound like a great strategy, but the truth is that the more volatile an investment is, the less successful a portfolio will be over the long term.

Many people don't realize how seriously volatility can diminish returns. If I asked you whether you'd rather have an investment that had a fixed annual return of 3 percent over six years or a volatile investment with an average annual return of 6 percent over six years, you'd probably choose the more volatile but seemingly higher return. But let's look at the overall performance of both investments:

	Steady Return		
Year 1	$1,000,000	3%	$1,030,000
Year 2	$1,000,000	3%	$1,060,000
Year 3	$1,000,000	3%	$1,090,000
Year 4	$1,000,000	3%	$1,120,000
Year 5	$1,000,000	3%	$1,150,000
Year 6	$1,000,000	3%	**$1,180,000**

Figure 10

	Volatile Return		
Year 1	$1,000,000	-30%	$700,000
Year 2	$700,000	15%	$805,000
Year 3	$805,000	15%	$925,750
Year 4	$925,750	-40%	$555,450
Year 5	$555,450	25%	$694,313
Year 6	$694,313	55%	**$1,076,184**

Figure 11

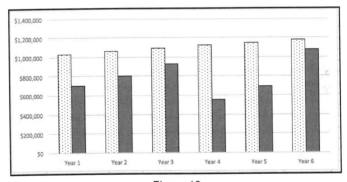

Figure 12

As you can see, the more volatile investment earns far less than the slow, steady, lower-return investment. By the end of the six-year period, the volatile position has earned just $76,184, while the steady return has earned $180,000.

Alternative investments like mortgage loans are a great complement to a portfolio because they are not correlated to the stock market and can be effective at strengthening a portfolio by reducing volatility.

A common strategy that I see repeated is investors removing some of their stock market gains during a bull market and placing them into either mortgage loans or mortgage loan funds. Then, during a bear market, they remain confident that a portion of their portfolio that is invested in mortgage loans will continue to provide income.

While I am not condoning an attempt to time markets, which is futile, let's look at how devastating volatility can be to an investment portfolio over time, and how reducing volatility ultimately means much larger gains.

Issues with Income

Stock market investments are not ideal for income generation; stocks are generally bought for growth and speculation. Worse, you can't control how the market is doing when you start liquidating stocks for income. That is when sequence of returns risk becomes a very big problem.

In the last section, we talked about the difference between a steady return and a volatile return. Let's see how that same $1 million investment is impacted when the investor needs to take a $25,000 annual income from it.

		Steady Return		
$1,000,000	3%	$1,030,000	-$25,000	$1,005,000
$1,000,000	3%	$1,030,000	-$25,000	$1,010,000
$1,000,000	3%	$1,030,000	-$25,000	$1,015,000
$1,000,000	3%	$1,030,000	-$25,000	$1,020,000
$1,000,000	3%	$1,030,000	-$25,000	$1,025,000
$1,000,000	3%	$1,030,000	-$25,000	$1,030,000
		Volatile Return		
$1,000,000	-30%	$700,000	-$25,000	$675,000
$675,000	15%	$776,250	-$25,000	$751,250
$751,250	15%	$863,938	-$25,000	$838,938
$838,938	-40%	$503,363	-$25,000	$478,363
$478,363	25%	$597,953	-$25,000	$572,953
$572,953	55%	$888,077	-$25,000	$863,077

Figure 13

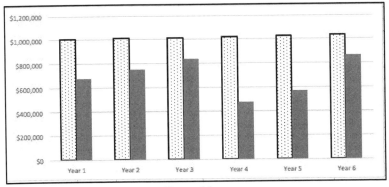

Figure 14

You can see that while we still have our $1 million principal in our "steady" investment and we've been taking out $25,000 in income, we've also been accumulating an additional $5,000 per year. Yet in our volatile investment, we've tapped into the principal and our balance has dropped below $900,000, despite an average annual return of 6 percent.

But, you may be thinking, what about stocks that pay a dividend? Wouldn't those be good for income? Well, that depends.

One of the biggest issues I have with dividends is that companies are not required to pay them and can revoke them at any time. For many years, Microsoft was under fire for deciding not to offer a dividend, despite having a profit.[31] While they reinvested this money into the business and the value of the stock grew, investors who were hoping for a dividend were out of luck. Not only are dividends not guaranteed, but dividend-paying stocks can go bust, or companies can simply suspend dividends, like Dunkin' Donuts and General Motors did in 2020.[32]

When investors look for dividend stocks to create regular income, they often change the parameters around their assessment of a stock. Instead of measuring risk and potential the same way they would a growth stock, they instead consider only the dividend potential. Worse, evaluating stocks this way can actually hurt overall returns as dividends can reduce stock prices.[33]

The most common way for investors to make money in the stock market is to sell shares for a higher price than the price at purchase. Sounds simple enough, but without the ability to time the market and without any meaningful control over company decisions, we have no way to create a positive environment for stock ownership. Worse, we, just as everyone else, are victims of the whims of the market—which means that even if a company is

---

[31]http://pages.stern.nyu.edu/~adamodar/New_Home_Page/articles/Microsoftdividends.htm
[32]https://www.nasdaq.com/articles/here-is-a-list-of-companies-that-have-suspended-dividends-or-stopped-stock-buybacks-in
[33]https://finance.zacks.com/dangers-buying-highdividend-stocks-1419.html

doing well by all measures, if consumer sentiment is against it, the price of its shares can plummet, just when we most need them to rise.

Stocks have their place in the portfolios of many. They offer opportunities for growth, intermittent income, and—when you're lucky—meteoric rises, if you're willing to take on some pretty major risks. Mortgage loan investments, on the other hand, remove the instability and costs of volatility while generating a predictable income/yield, with no exposure to market risks.

Mortgage Loans	Stocks
Represents a lien secured by real property. Lienholder is the primary interested party.	Shares represent ownership in a company. In a bankruptcy, preferred stockholders take priority.
Income is based on set payments with predetermined yield.	Income based on corporate profits (when companies pay dividends). Growth is based on share appreciation, reliant on investor interpretation.
Payments typically don't change.	Share price changes constantly.
Risk can be spread over many borrowers in many markets.	Risk is mitigated by diversification in industry, sector, and company.
Can control loans in portfolio.	Outside of voting rights, no control over the company.
Investor decides the yield at purchase.	Timing for buys and sells relies on predictions and advisors.

Funds

When you're looking toward the stock market to earn money, but want to play it safe, mutual or index funds might seem like a great compromise. With a mutual fund, instead of trying to find ways to pick the right stocks, you rely on a manager to buy and sell stocks to (hopefully) maintain fund performance. And that is where the problems begin.

Mutual Funds

The truth is, mutual fund performance generally underperforms the S&P 500.[34] That means the active managers who move positions in and out of the fund with the goal of creating a profitable fund have a performance that lags behind the S&P 500 index.

Making matters worse, mutual funds have fees that you pay, whether the fund is profitable or not. For many mutual funds, the fees include front-end and/or back-end loads, which are fees you pay when you buy or sell a stake in the fund. Even if you choose a fund with no buying or selling fee, also called a no-load fund, you still have what's called an expense ratio. This is a fund management fee, charged as a percentage against the fund's total assets.

Mutual fund fees can be especially egregious when they are held in a retirement account that has its own fees on top of the mutual fund fees. One of my biggest criticisms of the limited mutual funds that I was offered by my financial advisor were all the hidden fees and costs that I was paying to invest in those funds. This was within a 403(b) retirement account designed for teachers, which

---

[34]https://www.cnbc.com/2019/03/15/active-fund-managers-trail-the-sp-500-for-the-ninth-year-in-a-row-in-triumph-for-indexing.html

itself had high fees, which I was paying on top of the fees for the actual products within my plan.[35] Shouldn't teachers, who don't make much money to begin with, have access to the best funds with the lowest cost options available? Sadly, that wasn't the case, and one of the reasons I decided that I needed to take more control over my own wealth building for retirement.

If you plan on holding your mutual funds outside of a qualified account, you have another headache headed your way: unexpected taxes. At the end of each year, funds distribute a portion of the proceeds from trading on to their investors. These gains, which can be wildly unpredictable, are taxable to the investor when the fund is outside a retirement account. Because these gains can't be planned for in advance, they can easily result in higher tax implications, and less net profit.[36]

Index Funds

Index funds have grown in popularity in recent years. These are mutual funds with holdings that match or are similar to those of a chosen benchmark index. For example, an S&P 500 index fund might hold all the same positions that are on the S&P 500 index. Our recently ended, eleven-year bull market run made index funds seem like a great deal.

But index funds are a lot riskier than investors believe. First, many indices, which are the underlying benchmarks steering the positions in the fund, are heavily invested in a particular sector, such as the Vanguard

---

[35]https://www.fool.com/investing/2019/10/13/why-403b-plans-are-so-awful-so-often.aspx
[36]https://www.morningstar.com/articles/945237/stop-the-mutual-fund-capital-gains-distribution-madness

Information Technology index fund, which follows MSCI IMI/Info Tech 25-50 GR index.[37] So while investors with an index fund that has MSCI IMI/Info Tech 25-50 GR index as the benchmark might feel like they're well diversified, their holdings are actually all within one sector. As that sector loses value, so, too, will their portfolio, often without enough hedging against the losses.

Index fund investors also face the issue of rebalancing. In a normal portfolio, your asset allocation would be based on many factors, including your risk tolerance. The weight of each position within your portfolio changes every time the investments move up or down in value or you liquidate some portion of them. This means that your portfolio needs to be regularly rebalanced to ensure that the weight of each investment stays within the range it should be, based on your unique risk tolerance and other factors.

With an index fund, you can easily find that one underlying holding, as it grows within the fund, takes a much higher percentage of asset allocation than you would otherwise be comfortable with.

And of course, we should talk about the elephant in the room, which is the fact that index funds are extremely vulnerable to systemic risk. Some research has found that index funds may even contribute to systemic instability.[38] When you have a mix of assets, including equities, from a wide variety of industries, it is possible that some of your investments can hedge against losses when the market

---

[37]https://money.usnews.com/funds/mutual-funds/technology/vanguard-information-technology-index-fd/vitax#:~:text=The%20Vanguard%20Information%20Technol ogy%20Index,the%20majority%20of%20its%20performance.
[38]https://www.cfainstitute.org/-/media/documents/article/rf-brief/etfs-and-systemic-risks.ashx

begins to decline or when an index falls in value. But what happens if your investments are modeled against the very index that's falling?

Imagine buying an index fund in the 1990s. The fund you chose? One modeled after a precious metals index, which had seen an 82 percent gain the prior year. But by the end of the 1990s, the fund was worth less than half of what it was.[39] The same could happen with many of the index funds available today.

Where mortgage loans offer a steady stream of income, minimal fees for loan maintenance, a noncorrelated asset, and an asset "backed" by a home that's lived in by the owner, funds offer more risk, higher potential fees, and risks from improper diversification.

Mortgage Loans	Funds
No annual fees or commissions	Fees for managing the fund, fees for holding a fund within certain accounts, and fees for buying and selling some funds
Diversified among different homeowners in different regions	Diversified based on fund manager's performance of design of underlying benchmark
Predictable payments and yield based on purchase price	Valued at the end of the trading day, based on underlying position closing values (net asset value)

---

[39]https://www.morningstar.com/articles/1927/mutual-fund-notables-of-the-1990s

Bonds

Bonds are debt instruments that represent a loan the investor gives to a government or municipality. Through the bond, the issuer promises to repay the loan by a set maturity date and pay interest at the coupon rate.

Bonds are probably the most similar investment to mortgage loans, and the motivation between both bonds and mortgage loans is stable income that an investor can receive over time that is completely passive. Both are considered lower volatility (even though bonds are certainly not without risk), and the risk profile can be judged at purchase.

The problem I have found with bonds, including mortgage bonds, is that unless you are willing to purchase higher-risk junk bonds, it is hard to obtain low-risk yields above 5 percent.[40] As of the writing of this book, bond yields are averaging only 2 percent.

Another risk with bonds in the current ultralow yield environment is that investors essentially have two choices: commit to hold the bond to maturity for a very low interest rate, or sell it early. If you sell early during a rising yield environment, which we are undoubtedly entering, you can end up having to take a huge loss on your investment.

For example: You buy a thirty-year bond at 2 percent, and rates go up to 4 percent any time during your ownership period. If you decide you want to sell that bond, you would have to take a loss of up to 50 percent to match the yields in the bond market at the time you want to sell. I don't know about you, but that's not a loss I can stomach.

---

[40]https://www.thinkadvisor.com/2020/08/14/low-rates-arent-going-anywhere-heres-what-that-means-for-retirement-planning/

Mortgage Loans	Bonds
Secured by real property	Represent a promise by the issuer to pay back principal
Income based on set payments	Income paid when bond issuer can afford to
Payments typically don't change	When a bond issuer runs into trouble, they may miss a coupon payment
Investor decides yield at purchase	Yields determined by bond issuer or seller (in secondary market)
Additional liquidity by selling loan or partial (explained later in the book)	Additional liquidity through sale of bond, at a discount if interest rates have risen, potentially resulting in a loss of principal

Annuities

Another investment that has followed bonds in popularity during recent years are annuities, contracts issued by insurance companies that guarantee a specific fixed income to annuitants after principal is paid to the insurance company. Let's take a closer look at how they work.

Guaranteed Income: When and for How Long?

Annuities designed for ongoing income can pay that income in different ways. Some pay a guaranteed income for a limited term, some pay a guaranteed income until death of the annuitant, and some pay an ongoing income until the death of the last surviving joint annuitant.

The payment of this income comes after the annuity owner pays a premium, which is a lump sum of money paid in either a single contribution or in multiple payments.

In many ways, annuities are similar to mortgage loan investment, in terms of getting a steady, ongoing income. But unlike mortgage loan investments, annuity yields are very low and payments can vary, based on when you trigger them. For example, when you have a guaranteed minimum income benefit rider, the longer you wait to start the income, the higher your periodic payments will be.[41] Annuities also have administration and investment management fees as well as commissions.[42] Finally, annuity payments only occur when the insurance company is able to fulfill its promise of payment, a risk that some investors might not be willing to take.

Annuities have many built-in protections, such as inflation riders, which help to increase your future income to combat inflation. But many of these benefits come at an additional cost, which lowers the investment power of your principal.

---

[41]https://www.annuity.org/annuities/riders/gmib/
[42]https://www.fidelity.com/viewpoints/retirement/shoppers-guide-to-annuity-fees

Annuity Investments

Unless you buy a fixed annuity with a guaranteed return, you're likely to choose either a variable annuity or an indexed annuity. A variable annuity allows you the choice of an underlying mutual fund for your annuity premium to be invested in.

An indexed annuity requires you to choose an index, such as the Dow Jones Industrial Average or the S&P 500, and will credit your account with a return based on the performance of that index.[43]

General Liquidity

When buying an immediate annuity, payments can begin as soon as one month after purchase. Should you need more money from the annuity, you could find yourself paying a penalty if it's during the annuity's *surrender period*. With a mortgage loan, however, you could get additional liquidity either by selling the loan or by selling a partial interest in one or more of your loans (something I discuss in more detail in the More Ways to Invest in Mortgage Loans chapter).

Mortgage Loans	Annuities
Secured by real property	Relies on insurance company fulfilling terms
Payments start immediately	Payments might start immediately or may be deferred

---

[43]https://www.investor.gov/introduction-investing/investing-basics/investment-products/insurance-products/annuities

Able to be sold in full or partial to access principal	Can be surrendered, at a penalty
No ongoing fees	Ongoing fees for investment management, riders, administrative expenses, and more
Can control loans in portfolio	No control over underlying investments, other than selecting a fund or index
Payments don't vary	Payments may be higher the longer you wait before taking them

Evaluating the Risks of Mortgage Loan Investing

Risk is a part of every investment experience. There are no investments that are completely risk-free and few that combine low risk with a decent return that can beat inflation.

While we all interpret risks in different ways and we each have our own risk tolerance, I tend to categorize mortgage loan investments as one of the few investments that has minimal risks with great potential returns. Let's take a look at some of those risks so you can see for yourself.

Borrower Default

When considering mortgage loan investment risks, it would seem as if borrower default is the biggest risk. After all, your income comes from the homeowners making their monthly mortgage payments and eventually paying off their loans.

But as it turns out, this risk might not be something that needs to strike fear in an investor's heart for three reasons:

1. Homeowner default is statistically rare.
2. Mortgage loan investors can provide options for borrowers to help them get through short-term financial difficulties.
3. If no agreement can be made, mortgage loan investors retain the right to foreclose on a defaulted loan's collateral.

Now, let's talk about each of these factors in more detail.

The Statistics of Mortgage Default

In a normal economic time, during a "normal" year, delinquency rates on single-family homes are low. In fact, the delinquency rate for mortgages ninety days or more past due fell from 4.9 percent in January 2010 to 0.8 percent in December 2019.[44]

Of course, as the Great Recession and the COVID-19 Recession have taught us, normal is a gift we don't always get to enjoy. But a deeper look at actual delinquency and foreclosure rates during these events shows us that homes seem to be the last asset people are willing to lose.

It's been estimated that between 2007 and 2010, there were just 3.8 million foreclosures in the United

---

[44]https://www.consumerfinance.gov/data-research/mortgage-performance-trends/mortgages-90-or-more-days-delinquent/#mp-line-chart-container

States.[45] In quarter one of 2010, the delinquency rate for single-family residential mortgages reached its highest point, 11.54 percent. At the time, the unemployment rate was around 10 percent.[46] In quarter two of 2020, after months of a pandemic and lockdown orders and with an unemployment rate of 11.1 percent, the delinquency rate for single-family residential mortgages was just 2.49 percent.[47]

In part, the drastic difference between delinquency rates today versus around the Great Recession is likely due to changes in loan underwriting standards and lending regulations, as well as government intervention in the form of automatic forbearance—factors that will continue to benefit mortgage loan investors throughout the future years and potential economic upheaval.

Modifying Payments

Chances are good you've heard about banks offering mortgage loan modifications to borrowers dealing with resolvable financial issues. With these modifications, they can reduce the borrower's monthly payment and/or interest rate, extend the loan's maturity date, and add past-due balances to the principal amount owed.

Banks do this because it works. Between 2007 and 2016, more than 24 million nonforeclosure solutions were offered by the mortgage industry, rescuing millions from

---

[45]https://www.chicagofed.org/publications/chicago-fed-letter/2016/370#:~:text=As%20a%20result%20of%20the,were%20approximately%203.8%20million%20foreclosures.
[46]https://tradingeconomics.com/united-states/unemployment-rate
[47]https://fredblog.stlouisfed.org/2018/11/the-lowdown-on-loan-delinquencies/

foreclosure, keeping families in their homes and keeping payments rolling in.[48]

Our goal as lenders is simply to keep the loan payments coming in on a monthly basis, so common alternatives to foreclosure can include:

- short-term forbearance
- loan modification
- selling the house
- refinancing the house
- deed in lieu of foreclosure

These foreclosure alternatives are usually brought on by short-term financial hardships that prompt defaults. This can include difficult events such as:

- death in the family
- divorce
- job loss
- illness
- overwhelming debt, frequently due to medical bills

The key here is *short-term*. Federal law prevents lenders from filing a foreclosure until a borrower is 120 days delinquent on their loan, so this usually gives a loan servicer time to reach out to the borrower, assess the borrower's situation, and offer potential solutions.

Since loan servicers collect loan payments and communicate directly with the borrowers, investors should

---

[48]https://www.housingwire.com/articles/36455-hope-now-145-million-solutions-available-to-homeowners-in-2015/

not get involved. In many states, calling borrowers directly can be considered debt collection, which would require a state license. Personally, as an investor, I want as large a distance between myself and the borrower as possible.

Why do these alternatives work so well with homeowners? If you're used to dealing with tenants as a landlord and have had to evict—or threaten to evict—tenants, then you might not understand. As a landlord, I found that tenants generally viewed renting as a financial transaction. Their goal was to get the best unit for the lowest price, with the lowest amount down, and they were willing to move, even on short notice, for a better deal.

Also, the rental market was competitive. Many landlords would upgrade units and offer incentives like free rent to attract tenants; they'd even lower prices out of a need to fill units. Thus, many tenants weren't concerned about an eviction, in my experience, because they could always move to another rental.

Homeowners, however, are a completely different breed. Just think about how the process of buying a home starts—usually with a big down payment. People save money for years, handing over more money than they may ever have before, to buy a home. Once they move in, homeowners personalize their home and yard, and they expand their families, get pets, and make memories.

Besides that, over time, their equity in the property can grow to hundreds of thousands of dollars, making their home the most important investment many of them have. Homeowners have both a financial and emotional connection to their homes (even when they are underwater on value) and almost never walk away.

Foreclosure

While it doesn't happen often, there are borrowers who become so behind on mortgage payments that their lender files foreclosure. But, as I mentioned, this is infrequent, even during times of financial stress such as the Great Recession, when about 25 percent of homeowners were underwater, yet only 3.8 million ended up in foreclosure.[49,50]

Because we are secured lien holders, mortgage loan investors retain the right to foreclose on a property to reclaim the balance of the loan. As a lender, I am willing to provide alternatives to foreclosure if I see a clear resolution in sight. I don't want to displace borrowers unless absolutely necessary and all alternatives have been exhausted. But if no solution can be found, then sometimes foreclosure is the only answer. Just because a foreclosure case is filed doesn't mean that it will be completed; among the statistically small percentage of cases that are filed, even fewer actually make it to a foreclosure sale.

This is yet another reason I suggest that investors stick with owner-occupied, primary residences; homeowners are much less likely to allow them to go into foreclosure than they might a vacation or investment property.

Lending is a business. One of the biggest lessons I learned during thirteen years of real estate investing is that decisions should always be made based on the numbers,

---

[49]https://cnsmaryland.org/2020/05/19/a-decade-after-great-recession-home-values-in-some-communities-remain-underwater/

[50]https://www.chicagofed.org/publications/chicago-fed-letter/2016/370#:~:text=As%20a%20result%20of%20the,were%20approximately%203.8%20million%20foreclosures.

not on how I feel about a situation or my desire to shape an outcome. I strongly believe that I have a responsibility to the portfolio of loans I manage, and that means making sure timely payments continue to come in during the life of each loan.

While I want to help borrowers whenever possible, it's unreasonable for anyone to think they can stay in a home for a year or longer without paying a mortgage, taxes, or insurance. Sooner or later, everyone needs to face the reality of their situation, and delaying the inevitable just makes situations worse for everyone involved.

The key in mortgage loan investing is to have a large portfolio diversified over many borrowers in many markets in order to withstand any financial storm.

Falling Property Values

When you invest in real estate as a landlord or flipper, falling property values can be a great concern. After all, selling the property or leveraging the equity can be an important means of accessing capital and gaining profits. Falling property values threaten to undermine that completely.

From that perspective, mortgage loan investors don't need to be as concerned about falling property values. While I always look for equity in my purchases, since I don't own the property or need to use its equity as leverage or liquidity, the value of the property itself plays little role in my overall business model.

Instead, mortgage loan investors need to be concerned with how homeowners will react to falling property values. During the Great Recession, a common concern was that borrowers would abandon their homes as property values plummeted, and by March 2011, almost

30 percent of them were underwater or very close to it.[51] The term *strategic default* was coined by lenders to identify borrowers with negative equity who decided to just lock the doors of their home and walk away. Financial institutions were concerned that millions of homeowners would strategically default since there was no financial incentive for them to stay.

As it turns out, the concern over strategic default was overblown, which should give today's mortgage loan investors some additional confidence. J.P. Morgan Chase conducted a study in 2017 to learn about borrower behaviors and motivations during the financial crisis, and what they found was astounding.

Strategic default never happened.[52]

The study followed almost a half-million homeowners who received a home loan modification and found that in virtually every single case, the only borrowers who lost their homes were borrowers who had no financial ability whatsoever, either through themselves, a spouse, or family members, to continue to pay. In other words, default was tied to a fundamental drop in income, rather than a drop in property values or size of payments. Underwater borrowers stayed in their homes, continued to pay, and just waited for the housing market to rebound.

Why would they do this? Overwhelmingly because they loved their homes and wanted to stay in them! In

---

[51]https://www.corelogic.com/news/new-corelogic-data-shows-23-percent-of-borrowers-underwater-with-750-billion-dollars-of-negative-equity.aspx
[52]https://institute.jpmorganchase.com/content/dam/jpmc/jpmorgan-chase-and-co/institute/pdf/institute-mortgage-debt-reduction.pdf

2018, when almost two million homeowners still had negative equity, The New York Fed found that the primary reason underwater homeowners hadn't even considered strategic default was simple: they liked their homes and didn't want to lose them.[53]

When you think about it, everyone needs a place to live. Whether you're paying a mortgage or rent, you're paying living expenses. The extensive research done after the Great Recession shows us that homeowners would far prefer to keep paying for their homes rather than give them up to pay rent on a temporary dwelling they have no stake in, control of, or emotional tie to.

This data perfectly illustrates the importance of emotional equity in home ownership, which has proven to be even more powerful than financial equity. The mindset of a homeowner is completely different, because it involves *ownership*. Homeowners do not make rational, data-driven decisions about their homes. Their decisions are overwhelmingly emotional.

Furthermore, humans are essentially creatures of habit and familiarity who don't like change. Moving is difficult and expensive, and most people try to do it as rarely as possible. How could you find an investment that is better than this, with borrowers who are motivated to keep their mortgage current and in good standing, regardless of what happens in the economy and markets around them?

Interest Rate Changes

---

[53]https://www.marketwatch.com/story/why-do-underwater-homeowners-keep-paying-the-mortgage-2018-04-19

Interest rate risk is inherent with many investments. It describes the risk that when a fixed investment, such as a bond or CD matures, an investor may not be able to reinvest their principal at a similar rate if rates have fallen. Real estate investors face a different type of interest rate risk, as their expenses are driven up when they invest in properties by taking out mortgages during a high, or rising, interest rate environment.

Most commercial loans are balloons of about five years, meaning that investors are required to refinance their debt (and pay bank fees) upon the balloon's maturity, at the bank's discretion. If rates are increasing, investors could find themselves with a nasty surprise: increasing leverage costs that they cannot absorb by raising the rents. If banks sense systemic risk, they could decide not to refinance the loan at all, forcing the investor to either find a new bank or sell the property in the current market conditions. In a declining market with a neglected property, an investor could find themselves—pardon my language here—totally screwed.

For mortgage investors, interest rates, whether high or low, play no role in our ability to profit, even if we're reinvesting our principal when loans are paid off early and interest rates are extremely low. The reason we don't need to be concerned about interest rates is that we generally buy loans based on *yield*, not interest rate.

When mortgage loan investors calculate investment yield, we don't pay attention to the *borrower's* interest rate. Our only concern is *our yield*, which is based on the amount of each payment, the number of payments remaining, and the purchase price. Discount allows us to increase our desired yield to meet our investment requirement.

In addition, when rates fall, homeowners are more likely to refinance their loans, meaning we get paid back early. Depending on our purchase discount, an early payoff can drastically increase our investment ROI.

Out of the hundreds of billions of dollars of mortgage loans originated each year, there are wide varieties in the interest rates.[54] I review countless loans every year originated by smaller lending institutions or credit unions as far back as 1995, at or above 10 percent interest. Higher interest rates don't necessarily mean a higher-risk borrower, and they don't equal a higher yield. When a mortgage loan investor looks for a specific minimum yield, the calculation revolves around the cost of the loan and the remaining payments.

Let's take a look once more at the example we discussed in the Calculating Yield section. As you can see in Figures 15 and 16, the yield of the investment changes not because of interest rate, which isn't even a factor in the calculation, but based on the purchase price of the loan itself.

Number of payments	Monthly payment	Yield	Purchase price
132	$494.12	8%	$43,285.21

Figure 15

---

[54]https://www.consumerfinance.gov/data-research/consumer-credit-trends/mortgages/origination-activity/

Number of payments	Monthly payment	Yield	Purchase price
132	$494.12	12%	$36,125.48

Figure 16

No matter what interest rate homebuyers are paying, you can maintain the same yield with every new investment.

Risk may be an unavoidable reality of any investment worth having. Understanding the true nature of the risks associated with mortgage loan investing gives you the power to create hedges against them, such as diversifying the locations for your mortgage loans. Often, however, the very nature of this type of investment and its focus on yield create a far more hospitable environment for investors seeking low-risk and comfortable returns for a portion of their portfolio.

Making Your First Mortgage Loan Purchase

One question I receive more than any other is, "How do I find mortgage loans to purchase?" Unfortunately, it's probably the most challenging part of the process, because for some reason, the secondary market for mortgage loans is not an organized, efficient marketplace the way that real estate is.

The mortgage loan investment industry is overwhelmingly based on relationships. I have met the majority of the sellers that I purchase loans from through web searches, conferences, introductions from other investors, and through corporate brokers who are paid a fee on the total balance of the loans that are sold.

At least in the beginning, you must have a trusted professional (such as a CPA or attorney who has experience with mortgage loan investing) help you through purchases, because sellers expect fast due diligence and a smooth, quick transaction.

When I bought real estate for investment, the purchases were very organized and regulated by state law. The sellers were required to disclose what they knew about

93

the property, and a real estate agent could look out for my best interests. Experts reviewed both the property and the contract, and they could make revisions and recommendations as needed.

Those luxuries don't really exist when you are buying loans. It is completely up to you to look out for your own portfolio purchases and develop your own procedures and checklists if you decide not to invest in a mortgage loan fund.

Reputations are everything in the mortgage loan investment business, so being an easy buyer to work with will likely result in sellers reaching out to you when they need to move loans quickly, at a higher discount. I have obtained some really amazing deals in the past from sellers who were winding down investment funds and needed to liquidate all the assets before the fund could be officially closed.

With that said, I don't want to gloss over the fact that it's imperative to be very diligent and prepared. As the sellers I deal with will tell you, the worst thing a buyer can do is back out of a purchase for an arbitrary reason after leading the seller to believe they are prepared to close. Once a seller has a bad experience with a buyer, trust is lost, and the buyer will likely not hear from that seller again.

On that note, let's talk about how due diligence can make you a buyer that sellers love to work with.

But First, Yield

Before you start any due diligence, I highly recommend you ask the seller for their pricing expectations. If the seller's expectations don't meet your yield requirements, there is no reason to waste anyone's time. Also clarify whether the seller allows select bids on individual loans (referred to as *cherry picking*) or requires the purchase of the entire pool.

Due Diligence

In this section, I'm going to highlight for you some of the most important steps that I take to complete due diligence and find the best loans for my portfolio. The following is not intended to be an exhaustive list of every due diligence check that should be completed. Likewise, I can't guarantee that if you complete these steps, you will be successful.

While this may prove a good starting point in your education, it is not a complete list for you to follow. I highly recommend that you hire a knowledgeable attorney who understands note investment, and that you get an investing mentor before you begin to purchase loans. There are many ways investors can lose significant amounts of money in mortgage loan investment if they do not thoroughly understand the business.

I have purchased mortgage loans ranging in purchase price from $2,700 to $105,000, and I follow the exact same risk assessment on every loan to answer the question:

What is the likelihood this borrower will pay back the loan, and if they don't, am I comfortable with my recourse in the collateral property in order to be made whole?

Lending comes down to risk, and my responsibility as an investor overseeing my portfolio is to build a group of loans that has the highest yield return with the lowest risk profile. The more loans I own, the better I sleep at night, because unlike real estate, I have found that owning more loans provides a hedge against risk. I ask myself frequently, "What are the odds that all homeowners will stop paying their mortgage loans?" The answer is always zero.

Nevertheless, due diligence is paramount. There are many ways to get burned in a mortgage loan purchase, but having a solid checklist of items to double check can reduce much of the potential risk.

Understanding the Tape

When sellers market loans for sale, they include the important loan-specific data on a spreadsheet, which is referred to as a *tape*. Data on the tape usually includes:

- borrower name(s)
- address
- property value
- origination date
- monthly principal and interest payment
- interest rate
- servicer
- unpaid principal balance (UPB)
- maturity date
- recent pay history

Step 1: Analyze the Collateral Property

In my opinion, equity in the collateral property is probably the most important safeguard in a mortgage loan purchase. If default occurs and a solution cannot be worked out with the borrower, equity ensures that you should get your money back through a foreclosure sale.

Should the foreclosure sale have no bidders, the deed to the property reverts to the lender, which means you'll need to be comfortable getting your money back through the disposition of the property—either through selling, renting, or financing it.

To determine the equity present at the time of your investment, you need to know the difference between the outstanding mortgage(s) and the approximate value of the property. The outstanding mortgage amount(s) should be obtained from the seller. The property value might take a few more steps.

If you are buying a second lien, be sure to ask the seller for proof of the status of the first lien. You want to verify the balance, its current status, and whether it was ever modified. When I underwrite second liens, I combine the balance of the first and second lien and compare that total against the value of the property. More equity means a larger safety net.

Since investors can't get inside for an inspection, we have to rely on what we can see in pictures and online. To analyze the value of the collateral property, investors can use a desktop automated valuation model (AVM). AVMs offer a statistical value of the property that's based on how other, similar-area properties have sold.

If there is any confusion about the value of the property, or if it's in questionable condition, investors can order an exterior broker price opinion (BPO) from a local real estate agent. This involves the agent taking pictures of the property and using comparable properties and recent sales, along with a brief visual inspection of the property's condition to provide their opinion of the exterior appearance of current value. There are many companies that provide nationwide BPOs through their network of participant agents.

If you want to be very conservative with values, some investors reduce BPO values by 25 percent to reflect potential disrepair on the interior. If you're thinking about doing this, remember that completing a foreclosure on a homeowner is rare.

You might already be thinking that if you pull up an address on Google Maps and see that a property's exterior appearance is questionable, that it's not worth investing in. The issue of property appearance is much more nuanced than that.

In general, I try to avoid properties in complete disrepair because in my experience, the outside of a property usually reflects the condition of the interior. Thus, I like to see pride of ownership in the home, but a poorly maintained home does not mean a borrower is ready to relinquish ownership. In other words, a poorly maintained home may still be loved by its owner and the owner may have no desire to lose the property or move.

I have purchased loans on homes that appeared to be in below-average condition, and inherited borrowers that never missed a payment. This is just one reason why an investor's due diligence risk assessment must rely on many data points to build a picture of the borrower; the collateral property is only one of them.

If the property looks to be in below-average condition and everything else looks good, an investor may want to overlook the condition and make the investment, anyway. If, however, the collateral property is a structure that the investor would never be willing to take back after a foreclosure sale under any circumstances, they should pass. I always consider the worst-case scenario before purchasing a loan.

Step 2: Analyze the Loan Data

I have learned the hard way that you should always verify the information your seller provides to you on the tape. Sellers typically manage hundreds if not thousands of loans, and sometimes they make mistakes. The responsibility to verify all data is always the purchaser's.

Trust, But Verify

First and foremost, investors should review a current pay history from the loan servicer to verify the UPB of the loan, since this is the amount that helps determine the yield and drives the price of the investment. Additionally, investors should review all the monthly payments on the pay history, looking for any abnormalities that they need to ask the seller about. These can include a short, onetime history of late payments resulting from a temporary setback, or a repetitive problem with late payments that would require a larger discount.

While I review the pay history, adding up every single payment to verify the data is not necessary as long as the loan was serviced by a third party servicer. The seller should guarantee the UPB as part of the purchase contract.

Next, investors should double-check the data on the pay history against the data on the tape to verify the monthly payment amount and whether the loan includes escrows for taxes and insurance.

After that's done, investors should double-check the number of remaining payments by using an amortization software or financial calculator to make sure their calculations match what the seller is advertising.

Be very careful with loans that have been self-serviced, due to the risk of the borrower disputing the pay history after you have purchased the loan. One way to avoid disputes is to have the seller request the borrower sign and notarize an *estoppel affidavit*, which would stipulate the amount owed just prior to the loan sale.

Evaluating Lenders

One of the significant benefits of mortgage loan investing is that loan origination is completed by financial institutions held to high regulatory standards when it comes to underwriting, lending, and documentation. But not every home loan is underwritten by a financial institution. Some are originated by private lenders or are seller financed.

Investors should use extreme caution with seller-financed or privately originated loans. These should be carefully reviewed by an attorney who specializes in lending in the state the loan was originated. An improperly originated loan that did not follow all required state and federal laws and requirements could be deemed unsecured, uncollectable, or could even open up the investor for expensive litigation and liability.

Step 3: Analyze the Borrower

Although the property is the lender's collateral, and equity is the biggest safeguard, the borrowers and their financial ability to pay are the most important predictors of success in any mortgage loan purchase. To find out more about the occupants and their ability to pay, investors can subscribe to skip trace tools that provide data about the occupants of the property, as well as their ages.

Knowing that multiple working-age people live in a property is a good sign that there are several streams of income, but more than that, it can also show there are multiple generations of family living in a property, which is a great sign of emotional connection and can indicate a hesitance to move after putting down roots.

Next, investors should ask the seller for a copy of the borrower's credit report. This will not only show you the status and balance of the first lien and the borrower's FICO score, but also give you information about their other debts and their overall credit history and payment habits.

Before buying a loan, many investors review the borrower's credit to make sure it meets their minimum required score. In my opinion, the pay history of a loan is a more important indicator of potential risk. Borrowers can get in trouble with medical costs or other debts, but still want to keep their homes and make consistent payments. A loan with a solid pay history and high equity owned by a borrower with a lower credit score usually is a good opportunity for a larger discount and higher yield.

Finally, investors can check previous bankruptcy filings on Public Access to Electronic Court Records (PACER), available at www.pacer.uscourts.gov.

Bankruptcy filings are public knowledge and can be searched and reviewed. If a borrower has a recent bankruptcy filing, there will be valuable information that can be added to an investor's due diligence file. PACER has details about the debtor's employment, income, and intentions regarding their personal residence, making it a valuable resource for investors. Searchers must have an account to review PACER records, and there is a charge of $0.10 per viewed page.

Although information included in bankruptcy filings is public knowledge and can be searched, I strongly recommend that you review with an attorney your legal rights and responsibilities when viewing these documents.

Step 4: Analyze the Loan Documents

Reading through loan documents may not seem like a fun way to spend an evening, but it's a good idea for investors to do as part of their due diligence efforts.

When reading the loan documents, investors should verify that the most important data matches between the tape and the loan documents. This should include the borrower(s), property address, amount of the loan, origination and maturity dates, interest rate, monthly payment, and due dates.

Finally, investors should always check signatures, notarization on the mortgage or deed of trust, and loan modifications, if they exist (more about this on page 107). It's not impossible to discover unsigned loan documents, and those are probably loans investors want to avoid unless they first discuss their rights and legalities with a foreclosure attorney in the state where the loan was originated.

Let's talk about each of the loan documents in more detail, to give you a better sense of what to look for.

The Promissory Note

Mortgage loan investing is frequently referred to as *note investing*, because the borrower's signature on the promissory note is a legal promise to repay the lender according to the terms of the loan, including:

- the amount of the loan
- the interest rate, and whether it is fixed or adjustable
- the term of the loan and maturity date
- the monthly payment and due date
- late-charge guidelines
- other payment-related terms, such as a prepayment penalty or a balloon payment

Notes generated by financial institutions generally contain similar language and standardized provisions based on each state's laws.

It's important for investors to possess the original signed, wet-ink copy of the note, because in many states it is required to initiate a foreclosure. If the original note is lost, though, don't fret. In most cases, you can obtain a *lost note affidavit* from the prior owner of the loan or the party that lost the original copy. To understand what can and can't be done with a lost note and/or lost note affidavit, review the issue with a foreclosure attorney in the state the property is located.

The Mortgage or Deed of Trust

The mortgage or deed of trust document is the lender's security instrument, and it is recorded with the county as a lien against the property. These documents both identify the collateral property and include rights and requirements for the lender and borrower. In most cases, the documents specify that the borrower cannot sell or refinance the property without having the lien released. If the borrower defaults on the loan in any way described in the security instrument, the mortgage or deed of trust will include specific language that addresses how the lender may foreclose on the collateral property and sell it publicly in accordance with applicable state law.

Mortgages are typically used as security instruments in *judicial foreclosure states*, in which foreclosure cases must go through the legal system and be approved by a judge. Deeds of trust are mainly used in *nonjudicial foreclosure states*, in which a trustee is given the power to publicly sell the property without court approval.

Remember that each state's foreclosure process is unique, and seeking the guidance of a foreclosure attorney in the state in which the loan is located is imperative. Never attempt to file a foreclosure on your own. It is a highly complex process that, if not completed properly, can set a lender up for many different legal liabilities.

It's commonly believed that if a borrower defaults, the lender is entitled to take possession of the property. This is not true.

If no bidders bid on the property at the foreclosure sale (most commonly because more is owed to the lender than the property is worth), *only then* will it become property of the lender. The foreclosure process only allows the lender to be repaid what is owed to them. If the property sells for more at auction than what is owed, the excess funds will go to any junior lien holders and ultimately the borrower. In my experience, it is exceedingly rare for borrowers to walk away from equity in their home by losing it at a foreclosure sale.

Unsecured Loans

If there is no mortgage or deed of trust securing the debt, a loan is referred to as *unsecured*. Personal loans, credit cards, and peer-to-peer loans made through lending websites such as Lending Club are examples of unsecured loans, because there is no underlying collateral for the lender to seize if the borrower defaults.

While unsecured loans may be a valid option for some, mortgage loan investing creates security for investors since they retain the legal right to sell the collateral property if they are not repaid by the borrower according to the terms in the note. This is what makes mortgage loan investments lower risk. Without that security, unsecured loans lose their appeal for my portfolio.

Assignments and Allonges

When a loan is sold to a new lender, the note and mortgage must be transferred. This is a relatively simple process that involves two documents.

To transfer the note, either an *endorsement* or an *allonge* is used. An endorsement is similar to a check endorsement and is usually stamped on the original note and signed over to the new owner. An *allonge* is a separate

LIENLORD

document attached to the note. It usually uses the term *pay to the order of:*, names the buyer's entity, and includes the seller's signature.

The mortgage or deed of trust is transferred via a document called an *Assignment of Mortgage (AOM),* or *Assignment of Deed of Trust,* which is a simple, one-page document that shows the new lender's information, including the entity name and address. This document is recorded on title with the county and provides a public record of who currently owns the lien.

At this point in the process, your goal is to look into past transfers to check the assignment and allonge chain to make sure there is a complete transfer history of ownership on the loan. The goal is to make sure there are no missing documents (referred to as breaks) in the AOM or allonge chains. If there are, investors can either approach the seller about the missing documents and ask them to procure them, or discuss the issue with an attorney in that state.

In some cases, you can still legally foreclose if you are missing AOMs or allonges, but this isn't always true, so you want to make sure you verify the documents with an attorney. Another option is to have your collateral custodian reach out to the previous lender for you to obtain any missing documents.

Loans that are missing collateral documents usually sell at a deeper discount. As long as you discuss the issue with an attorney prior to your purchase and are comfortable with your legal options, these loans may represent a good opportunity, albeit a lower resale value.

Investors can (and, in my opinion, should) outsource the collateral part of the business to a corporate collateral custodian. They are experts in the field and can handle all aspects of the collateral document business for you, including storing collateral, generating documents, recording documents, shipping files, and even signing on your behalf under a power of attorney so you can focus on your core business: buying more loans and increasing your monthly cash flow.

A Special Note on Loan Modifications

While forbearance agreements help borrowers who are experiencing a temporary financial setback, we've discussed how loan modifications are a great way for lenders to help homeowners remain in place following a financial hardship in which the borrower would benefit from loan terms that are permanently changed. Because of this, investors may notice some of the loans they purchase have been modified by a prior lender.

Loan modification isn't a verbal agreement. It involves important documents that alter the terms of the original loan and can include changes to the:

- loan balance
- monthly payment
- interest rate
- due date
- maturity date

Investors need to first ensure that the tape accurately reflects the modified loan terms. Then, they should look to see if a *balloon* (requirement for the borrower to pay off the loan in a lump sum prior to full amortization) has been added to the agreement. While not always legally required, these documents should be notarized.

And that's it. Those are the steps I take for pre-bidding due diligence. Once again, I highly recommend you speak with an attorney before finalizing your due diligence process.

Bidding on Loans

After completing all the due diligence that can be done for free, investors will have narrowed the field and found loans they want to bid on. These loans will have:

- a flexible enough price to meet yield requirements
- satisfactory collateral property
- correct loan data on the tape
- necessary collateral documents
- on-time pay history
- borrowers with a high likelihood of continued payment

One of the things you'll need to consider next is how much to bid. Initially, you will have had a yield target in mind, but now, knowing more about the loan, borrower, and property, you may want to adjust your yield pricing. The factors that will impact the yield you choose include:

- the amount of equity exceeding the loan balance(s)
- whether the loan is a first or second lien
- pay history

- whether the property is in a judicial or nonjudicial state
- status of the collateral file
- existing modifications
- borrower down payment at modification
- borrower credit score
- bankruptcy status
- motivation of the seller

When you've verified all information and determined your target yield and purchase price, you should complete a few final checks before bidding on the loan(s).

Final Checks

When investing in a first lien, reviewing a lender's title policy and proof of homeowners insurance is critical. A lender's title policy protects the lender against title problems or claims that could affect the secured status of their first-position lien. Lender's title policies are primarily used for first liens and are less common for second liens originated as HELOCs; that is why reviewing the title prior to purchase is so important. Without a title report, you have no way of knowing whether the lien you are buying is in second or third position.

A homeowner's hazard insurance policy covers the collateral property against damage. Prior to purchase, investors should ask the seller for a copy of the borrower's homeowners insurance information. After purchase, the loan servicer should request to be added to the borrower's insurance policy as:

- **Mortgagee:** This requires the insurance company to provide notification if the policy is cancelled.
- **Additional insured:** This reflects the investor's interest in the property as a secured lien holder.
- **Loss payee:** This requires the homeowner to get the investor's signature on any claim monies used to rebuild the property, so the borrower cannot run off with a large check and not rebuild the collateral.

In some cases, a borrower will not have insurance on the property. If they don't have insurance, your servicer can *force place* insurance, which means placing a policy that protects the collateral for your interests.[55] Since the loan documents require the borrower to insure the property, they will be required to pay for the forced-placed policy, but the policy can be only for the amount the borrower owes on the loan. Charges for the cost of the policy can be added to the borrower's loan balance.

Placing a Bid

The tape you received will have a deadline for bids. On or before the deadline, you can submit what's called an *indicative bid*. This is an offer based on several conditions, which you should disclose to the seller.

My indicative bids are typically contingent on a title report and an exterior BPO if I have any doubt on value.

---

[55]https://www.dfs.ny.gov/consumers/help_for_homeowners/insurance/force-placed_insurance

Bids are usually submitted simply by email on a spreadsheet. Your bid may be higher or lower than you initially thought, based on the information you discovered during your due diligence. In other words, you may find that you want a bigger discount and a higher yield for loans that you now feel are higher risk or have a lower-valued collateral property.

I always disclose to the seller any pertinent information I found in my due diligence that is affecting my bid, especially if I bid for less than I originally expected.

Each investor can bid only once, and if another investor bids a higher percentage of a loan's unpaid balance, they will usually win the sale—unless the seller likes you so much, they would rather award the bid to you. Don't underestimate the value of reputation and relationships in the mortgage industry.

Title Review

Once the seller notifies you that your bid has been accepted, you should immediately clear up any remaining contingencies so you can close the deal as quickly as possible.

As a final step, and just prior to closing, investors should order a title report on the property. *I cannot stress enough how important this is.* Among other information, this will allow you to verify:

- the current owner
- whether the property is currently in foreclosure
- whether there are any other liens or encumbrances on the property that could interfere with your ownership
- the annual property tax rate

- the presence of any unpaid taxes, tax liens, or tax deed sales
- whether the loan is secured by a lien on title and has not been released by the lender
- if the lien is in either first or second position
- any prior loan modifications recorded on title
- all the recent documents that have been recorded on title

Since this is such an important check, and title issues can be complex, beginning investors should pay to have a real estate attorney review the title report and supporting documents. There is nothing more important than ensuring you're buying a secured lien without any major title issues.

When reviewing a title report for a second lien purchase, be sure to review any loan modifications that were completed on the first lien. These are not always reflected on a credit report and can change your equity position if the first lien added a deferred balance to the end of the loan that has to be paid off upon sale or refinance.

Reviewing the Loan Sale Agreement

The loan sale agreement (LSA) is the final document representing the sale of the loan from the seller to the purchaser. You can review a sample LSA at the SEC website.[56]

---

[56]https://www.sec.gov/Archives/edgar/data/1466225/00011931 2511055174/dex108.htm

An LSA is a sophisticated, legally binding document. When you're starting off in mortgage loan investing, it's critical to have the LSA between you and the seller reviewed by an attorney who understands mortgage loan investment. At the very minimum, the LSA should provide complete clarification about:

- **Funding and cutoff dates:** These deadlines clarify the date the loan purchase must be funded and the date after which all incoming payments are rightfully owned by the purchaser.
- **Borrower payment during the purchase process:** Your LSA must specify how payments are handled after the sale occurs, and should include a procedure for forwarding borrower payments to the purchaser if funds are received by the seller after the cutoff date.
- **Representations and warranties:** Is the seller guaranteeing the original note and allonges, as well as a complete assignment chain? A secured lien? A certain lien position? If you discover otherwise, what recourse is the seller providing to you and with what deadline?
- **Costs:** Spells out who pays for the preparation and recording of the assignment and allonge to the purchaser.
- **Servicing transfer:** Specifies how quickly the transfer of servicing should take place, and what happens if it doesn't occur in that amount of time. Also covers the procedure for the servicer notifying the borrower of the sale of the loan, in accordance with federal law.
- **Dispute resolution:** Allows buyer and seller to agree to waive the right to a jury trial and name the

venue for filing disputes, or to choose mediation/arbitration only.

- **Schedule A:** An attachment to the agreement that includes the loan data, such as borrower name, address, last payment, payment amount, UPB, and purchase price. The UPB is the most important data point, and the seller should warrant that you are purchasing that specific amount of debt.

Many sellers use similar LSAs, but don't be afraid to ask questions or have the seller add in language specific to an individual loan purchase if needed. LSAs are generally negotiable contracts that can be changed or altered depending on the individual characteristics of the deal. Each purchase is a little different.

Funding the Loan Investment

Sellers always expect you to wire funds for a loan purchase directly to their account. This is not something I'm comfortable doing unless I have an established business relationship with the seller. Instead, I like to use an attorney as a third-party escrowee, hopefully in the state where the loan is located.

The procedure for using a third-party escrowee is simple, and looks like this:

- The seller ships the loan file to the attorney. The file includes an assignment of mortgage and allonge to the buyer's entity.
- The buyer wires the funds to the attorney.
- The attorney reviews the file, and when everything is found to be satisfactory, the funds are released by the attorney to the seller.

115

- Once the funds are released, the attorney ships the entire collateral file to the buyer's collateral custodian.

I generally offer to pay the escrow fee since I am being protected by it, and even allow the seller to choose the attorney if they prefer.

After the deal is closed, the buyer's servicer will send out a letter to the borrower, letting them know of the identity of the new owner and the location to send payments.

More Ways to Invest in Mortgage Loans

By now, you probably have a much better idea what role mortgage loan investing might play in your overall portfolio allocation and future income plans.

Now, let's go a step further and talk about some alternative ways to invest in mortgage loans and some different types of loans to invest in. As I walk through these steps, please remember that my goal is to introduce you to these concepts and expand your understanding of what's possible in your portfolio. Please consult with a CPA, attorney, financial advisor, and IRA plan custodian before taking action and making any investments.

Baby Steps: Partial Loan Purchases

What if you're not ready to purchase a whole loan? Whether you're concerned about concentrating that much capital in a single investment or you simply don't have enough money to take such a big step, you might instead start by purchasing just part of a loan.

A *partial loan purchase* is a great way to test the mortgage loan investing model with a lower capital contribution while learning the fundamentals. A partial loan purchase contract has three parties: the seller, the buyer, and the borrower. Partial loan sales occur when a seller wants to raise capital from a mortgage loan investment, but doesn't want to sell an entire loan. Let's take a look at how it works.

Example

In Figure 8, showed you this loan I bought in California:

Purchase price	$21,000.00
UPB (unpaid principal balance)	$27,376.22
Monthly payment	$351.84
Payments remaining	104
Yield	14.18%
Total collected over life of loan	$36,591.36

If, after buying this loan, I found that I needed to raise $10,000 and didn't want to sell the entire loan, I could sell a portion of the payments to another investor at an agreed-upon yield.

For example, let's say I am willing to give the purchaser a 9 percent yield. With our financial calculator, we can figure out how many payments I need to sell to the buyer to return a yield of 9 percent:

N: number of payments	PMT: monthly payment	I/YR: desired yield	PV: purchase price
Unknown	$351.84	9%	-$10,000

Figure 17

By entering the data and then pressing the N key, you will get an answer of thirty-two. That means I need to sell the buyer a total of thirty-two payments to provide a 9 percent yield. Let's look at an actual amortization schedule to provide even more detail.

Partial purchase price	$10,000
Monthly borrower payment	$351.84
Buyer's yield	9%
Number of payments required to yield 9%	32
Total amount collected by buyer	$11,258.88

Figure 18

LIENLORD

Compounding Period:	Monthly
Nominal Annual Rate:	9.000%

Cash Flow Data - Loans and Payments

	Event	Date	Amount	Number	Period	End Date
1	Loan	07/14/2020	10,000.00	1		
2	Payment	08/14/2020	351.84	31	Monthly	02/14/2023
3	Payment	03/14/2023	381.49	1		

TValue Amortization Schedule - Normal, 365 Day Year

	Date	Payment	Interest	Principal	Balance
Loan	07/14/2020				10,000.00
1	08/14/2020	351.84	75.00	276.84	9,723.16
2	09/14/2020	351.84	72.92	278.92	9,444.24
3	10/14/2020	351.84	70.83	281.01	9,163.23
4	11/14/2020	351.84	68.72	283.12	8,880.11
5	12/14/2020	351.84	66.60	285.24	8,594.87
2020 Totals		**1,759.20**	**354.07**	**1,405.13**	
6	01/14/2021	351.84	64.46	287.38	8,307.49
7	02/14/2021	351.84	62.31	289.53	8,017.96
8	03/14/2021	351.84	60.13	291.71	7,726.25
9	04/14/2021	351.84	57.95	293.89	7,432.36
10	05/14/2021	351.84	55.74	296.10	7,136.26
11	06/14/2021	351.84	53.52	298.32	6,837.94
12	07/14/2021	351.84	51.28	300.56	6,537.38
13	08/14/2021	351.84	49.03	302.81	6,234.57
14	09/14/2021	351.84	46.76	305.08	5,929.49
15	10/14/2021	351.84	44.47	307.37	5,622.12
16	11/14/2021	351.84	42.17	309.67	5,312.45
17	12/14/2021	351.84	39.84	312.00	5,000.45
2021 Totals		**4,222.08**	**627.66**	**3,594.42**	
18	01/14/2022	351.84	37.50	314.34	4,686.11
19	02/14/2022	351.84	35.15	316.69	4,369.42
20	03/14/2022	351.84	32.77	319.07	4,050.35
21	04/14/2022	351.84	30.38	321.46	3,728.89
22	05/14/2022	351.84	27.97	323.87	3,405.02
23	06/14/2022	351.84	25.54	326.30	3,078.72
24	07/14/2022	351.84	23.09	328.75	2,749.97
25	08/14/2022	351.84	20.62	331.22	2,418.75

	Date	Payment	Interest	Principal	Balance
26	09/14/2022	351.84	18.14	333.70	2,085.05
27	10/14/2022	351.84	15.64	336.20	1,748.85
28	11/14/2022	351.84	13.12	338.72	1,410.13
29	12/14/2022	351.84	10.58	341.26	1,068.87
2022 Totals		**4,222.08**	**290.50**	**3,931.58**	
30	01/14/2023	351.84	8.02	343.82	725.05
31	02/14/2023	351.84	5.44	346.40	378.65
32	03/14/2023	381.49	2.84	378.65	0.00
2023 Totals		**1,085.17**	**16.30**	**1,068.87**	
Grand Totals		**11,288.53**	**1,288.53**	**10,000.00**	

ANNUAL PERCENTAGE RATE The cost of your credit as a yearly rate.	FINANCE CHARGE The dollar amount the credit will cost you.	Amount Financed The amount of credit provided to you or on your behalf.	Total of Payments The amount you will have paid after you have made all payments as scheduled.
9.000%	**$1,288.53**	**$10,000.00**	**$11,288.53**

Figure 19

Here's a simple breakdown of the process:

- The buyer wires the seller the $10,000.
- The seller assigns the loan to the buyer and sets up the partial contract with the loan servicer so the next thirty-two payments of $351.84 are paid directly to the buyer.
- The seller then has the $10,000 they need for their investing purposes, and the buyer has a short, inexpensive introduction to mortgage loan investing with a 9 percent yield.
- After the thirty-two payments are made, the loan reverts back to the seller, who has the right to collect the remaining seventy-two payments.

- If the loan is paid off early, all the payments received by the buyer are amortized along with the buyer's interest rate and the total amount the buyer invested to determine the refund due to the buyer. This is tracked by the loan servicer.

Partial loan purchases are a win for both parties: the seller gets a cash infusion and still gets to keep the tail end of the loan, and the buyer gets a solid yield on a lower-risk investment, since the seller isn't going to do anything, or allow anything, to jeopardize their investment in the remaining loan payments.

With that said, it's still important to do the same due diligence on a partial loan purchase as you would a full loan purchase. The difference with a partial is that there is no competitive bidding process. The seller will review all the data with you, explain all aspects of the loan purchase, and allow you to ask as many questions as you need to feel comfortable with the investment.

Partial Loan Purchases FAQ

Who owns the loan during the partial sale period?
The loan will be assigned to the buyer during the period that the buyer is collecting payments, and will be assigned back to the seller once the buyer receives their entitlement.

What happens if the borrower defaults during a partial?
Most partial loan sale contracts allow the seller to do one of the following in case of a borrower default:

- Buy back the loan.
- Continue to make the payments to the buyer.

- Begin legal proceedings at the seller's expense.

Remember, the seller retains the right to many tail-end payments in the loan, so they have a vested interest in making sure the borrower keeps the loan current.

How is the loan serviced during the partial sale period?
Once the contract is signed and forwarded to the loan servicer, the loan is set up as a partial in the servicer's system. The servicer tracks the balance of the buyer's partial payment entitlement.

Which party pays the servicing fee?
The net monthly payment, after servicing, is used for the buyer yield calculations.

What paperwork is required?
The seller and buyer sign a contract that covers the partial loan purchase, which includes amortization schedules for both the buyer and the borrower, covering the number of payments sold.

What if the loan is paid off early?
All the payments the buyer already received would be entered into an amortization schedule, along with the buyer's interest rate and the total amount the buyer invested to determine the refund due to the buyer. The loan servicer tracks this data on a monthly basis and would distribute the correct amounts between the buyer and the seller.

What if the borrower makes irregular payments (pays more each month than they are required to)?

Additional principal payments reduce the amount owed to the buyer, since the principal amount is paid back faster. The loan servicer tracks the amount due to the buyer each month during the partial contract.

What are the advantages of partial note purchases?
- Seller provides all due diligence for the buyer's review.
- Seller steps in and rectifies the situation if the borrower defaults.
- Buyer legally owns the loan during the partial.
- Capital commitment is reduced.
- Investment term is reduced.
- It's a relatively simple process with high yields and lowered capital needs, making it great for IRAs.

Buying Second Liens

When buying a loan, investors can choose whether to buy a lien in the first or second position. Title companies use the old title expression, *first in time, first in right,* to decide which lien gets paid off first when a property is sold or liquidated. This means that, with some exceptions, liens recorded first are paid off first, while second and third liens are paid off with any remaining funds.

There are two reasons investors traditionally believe that second liens are riskier:

- If the borrower defaults, either lender can foreclose, but the lender in first-position lien will be paid first. If the first lien forecloses, it can unsecure the second-position lien at foreclosure sale.

- Owning second liens can pose a risk when markets fall and home values drop, potentially unsecuring the second lien due to loss of equity.

In theory, both of these concerns are valid, but in my experience, due to the power of emotional equity, they have proven to be unfounded. Let's explore why.

Busting the Second Lien Danger Myth

The most common type of second lien loan today is a home equity line of credit, or HELOC, which allow borrowers who have equity in their homes to go to a financial institution and take out a second mortgage on their home.

For example, let's say a borrower has a $150,000 first mortgage balance on their home worth $250,000. In order to add on an extra bedroom to their home, they take out a $40,000 HELOC. The borrowers will now have two mortgage payments each month, usually to two different lenders.

HELOCs tend to be structured differently, with an initial draw period, during which the borrower can use the credit line like a checkbook and only pay interest on the amount of money they use. At the end of the prescribed draw period, the loan converts to a repayment period, during which borrowers usually make regular monthly payments to repay the balance with interest.

HELOCs are primarily used for home improvements.[57] This is not generally a move made by someone who is ready to lose their home. In fact, second

---

[57] https://www.housingwire.com/articles/43830-heloc-use-is-on-the-rise/

liens can be preferable to buying a first lien. Why? Because second liens usually are characterized by:

- higher property values
- more financially sophisticated, higher-income borrowers able to withstand recessions
- lower loan purchase prices
- more frequent refinancing
- less competition from other buyers/investors

Other benefits of second lien purchases include:

- taxes and insurance escrowed/monitored by the first lien servicer
- the ability to monitor the status of the first lien
- risk can be spread amongst many more loans
- higher yields and greater discounts

Because of my experiences in real estate investing during the 2008 recession, I expected my inventory of second liens to have a higher default rate during the COVID-19 recession of 2020. I was shocked when that didn't happen. Not only did it not happen, I found that the few defaults I had were on first liens! I suspect this is because the borrower's income is usually tied to the value of the home, and most first liens are on properties with values under $150,000.

So while most people think that second liens are riskier, lower-income borrowers are more often living paycheck to paycheck and are more likely to run into financial trouble during economic downturns.

Another benefit I have found to investing in second liens is that first lien servicers are usually handling tens of thousands of loans, and they are usually understaffed and slower to react to borrower default. If I keep an eye on the first lien status, it allows me to act first to best control the outcome if there is a first lien default. Better yet, there are many ways an investor can protect a second-position lien, and to date, I have never lost a second lien to foreclosure.

Even if you don't want to monitor the performance of the first lien, you will be notified of any adverse actions because in most states, first lienholders are required to notify second lienholders in the event of foreclosure action.

With second liens, time is on the investor's side. Following every scheduled payment, the first lien balance is reduced as principal is paid back; at the same time, the value of the property is increasing. This creates a constantly increasing equity position that benefits the borrower and protects the second lien lender.

Time Creates Equity

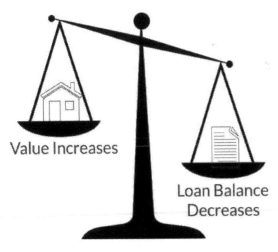

Value Increases

Loan Balance Decreases

Figure 20

Due Diligence on Second Liens

When underwriting junior liens and deciding whether to buy them, investors should ask the seller for proof of the status of the first lien to ensure it is current and in good standing.

They should also consider the *combined loan to value* (CLTV), which is the amount of equity above both the first and second liens. This is found by dividing the total UPB of the loans by the value of the property. Here's an example of a low CLTV scenario I'd be very comfortable with:

1 Full Equity Street, Anytown, USA

Estimated value: $400,000
First lien UPB: $225,000
Second lien UPB: $57,000
Combined mortgage loan debt: $282,000
Equity: $118,000
CLTV: $282,000/$400,000 = 70%

Here is a loan scenario that is less desirable due to a CLTV of more than 100 percent:

2 Riskier Street, Anytown, USA

Estimated value: $400,000
First lien UPB: $385,000
Second lien UPB: $57,000
Combined mortgage loan debt: $442,000
Equity: $15,000
CLTV: $442,000/$400,000 = 110%

In the last example, there is only $15,000 of equity coverage for the loan of $57,000. Simply as a conservative measure, I generally look for loans that have a CLTV under 80 percent. More equity means more security for both the borrower and the junior lien lender.

Some investors use *investment to value* (ITV) in place of CLTV. ITV represents what the investor paid for the loan instead of the UPB of the loan. It's calculated by dividing the purchase price of the loan by the value of the property.

The goal of any investor is to build as diversified and balanced a portfolio as possible. For mortgage loan investors, that means buying loans in markets across the country, in *both* first and second lien positions. Diversification lowers risk and second liens allow investors to spread their risk so much more.

From Nonperforming Loans to Reperforming Loans

Financial institutions originate billions in loans each year, yet foreclosure numbers average less than 1 percent.[58] Within that gap lies a special opportunity for some mortgage loan investors who want to turn nonperforming loans (NPLs), those which have gone at least ninety days without payment, into reperforming loans.

---

[58]https://www.attomdata.com/news/market-trends/foreclosures/attom-data-solutions-2019-year-end-u-s-foreclosure-market-report/

Why Banks Don't Foreclose

Financial institutions are in the lending business, not the collections business. These companies have a massive number of loans to service, and in my experience, they are not designed to effectively collect on delinquent loans. In most cases, they don't have employees with the knowledge and abilities needed to handle delinquencies.

Compounding this issue is the negative public perception issues facing banks that foreclose on borrowers, especially during times of recession. Most financial institutions don't want the bad publicity or legal and political scrutiny that comes with filing foreclosures and potentially evicting borrowers from their homes.

Finally, foreclosure is an expensive, lengthy process that in some states can take years if contested by the borrower. In many cases, especially with second liens, it is preferable for financial institutions to write down these loans as loss against their profits and sell them off at discount on the secondary market to a private fund that is willing and able to spend the time and money to file a foreclosure case and ultimately solve the delinquency problem.

Buying NPLs

Banking regulations typically require financial institutions to identify nonperforming loans on their books after ninety days of nonpayment.[59] Once they write the loan down as a loss, they don't continue to try to collect on the loan. Instead, they frequently sell off the loans to recoup what

---

[59]http://pubdocs.worldbank.org/en/314911450690270267/FinS AC-LoanClassification-Provisioning-Paper.pdf

money they can and put those funds back into circulation, making new loans and generating new fees.

In my experience as an investor in defaulted loans, by the time these loans are sold after being written down, the homeowner is frequently in a better financial situation and motivated to keep their home. I'm not the only investor with this experience, since there are many private investment funds that specialize in purchasing these NPLs and working with borrowers to modify the loans.

Although I have extensive experience in NPL investment, it is a much riskier investment model reliant on complex litigation in a constantly changing legal landscape with no guarantee of any profitable outcome. For that reason, I **strongly discourage** NPL investment for beginning investors who cannot handle the risk of a total loss of their invested capital.

The motivation behind filing a foreclosure case for an NPL is NOT to displace the borrower; it is simply to get them to resume paying. A foreclosure action requires the borrower to make a decision and address the debt prior to the foreclosure sale. About 60 percent of the time, these nonperforming loans end up with a borrower requesting and agreeing to a loan modification. Prior to modifying the loan, the lender requires the borrower to submit a detailed financial application.

The lender's goal in a modification is to create a loan that the borrower will not redefault on, so it's in the lender's best interest to modify the loan to terms that the borrower clearly can afford. Because the investor has purchased the loan at a significant discount, they can afford to pass on these savings to the borrower in the form of a favorably modified loan, creating a positive solution for all parties.

Once these loans are modified, they are commonly sold in the secondary market as *reperforming loans* (RPL). I regularly purchase RPLs, both first and second liens, and have found them, over time, to be strong investments. Here's why:

- Foreclosure is a very stressful experience for borrowers. It forces them to face the reality that they could lose their home, and once they resolve the foreclosure, they don't want to experience the stress of a foreclosure again.
- A foreclosure filing is embarrassing, since the publicly recorded foreclosure filing is reflected on websites like Zillow, which all of their neighbors can see.
- The bigger the down payment at loan modification, the larger the statement from the borrower that they want to stay in their home and the lower the likelihood of a redefault.
- Since NPLs are purchased anywhere from 20 to 65 percent of UPB, the sellers can afford to sell them with higher yields and deeper discounts since their business model involves flipping the loans to reinvest their capital.
- Borrowers tend to refinance these loans more frequently, due to the higher interest rates, rolling the balance of the second mortgage into just one loan. When that happens, the ROI skyrockets.

Buying Mortgage Loans in Active Bankruptcy

What if some of your preconceived fears and assumptions about mortgage loan investing just weren't true? Many of my original beliefs about the industry and borrower behaviors have proven to be completely wrong. One of the biggest surprises has been in second liens and reperforming loans. Another eye-opener has been the success I've found investing in mortgage loans in active Chapter 13 bankruptcy, the last option for struggling borrowers buried in debt who don't want to lose their homes.

Understanding Chapter 13

Many people are under the misconception that bankruptcy is the domain of the irresponsible, a belief that could certainly make someone less likely to want to buy a mortgage loan that's involved in an active bankruptcy.

Sadly, the number one reason for bankruptcy filings is medical debt, which played a role in about 66 percent of bankruptcy cases between 2013 and 2016.[60] While these borrowers may seem like a huge credit risk on paper, they still want and need to keep their homes, which is exactly what Chapter 13 bankruptcy was designed for.

Debtors who file Chapter 13 have regular income, and are given three to seven years to reorganize their financial affairs with a court-approved and monitored repayment plan. Creditors who have a collateralized loan, (like a car or a house) are secured creditors, meaning their

---

[60]https://www.businessinsider.com/causes-personal-bankruptcy-medical-bills-mortgages-student-loan-debt-2019-6

debt is secured by lien. Unsecured creditors without collateral in a Chapter 13 case are likely to get a greatly reduced amount repaid in the bankruptcy plan, if anything at all.

Mortgage loan investors are secured creditors, which means their debts are given priority over unsecured debt, and in most cases, the amount owed cannot be reduced. Under the federal bankruptcy code, borrowers who state their intention to retain their residence must normally bring their loan current during their bankruptcy plan. This means making regular payments required under the terms of their loan, *plus* repaying all arrears (unpaid interest during the period of default).

Borrowers must have their repayment plan (which usually spans sixty months) approved by the court. The goal is to have the borrower exit bankruptcy with their mortgage loan(s) current and in good standing.

Technically, borrowers who complete a Chapter 13 bankruptcy plan and receive a discharge from the court are no longer personally liable for their mortgage debt. Sounds scary, right? Not really, because the lien on the property remains, and the creditor retains the right to foreclose against the collateral property, even if the borrower is no longer personally liable for the debt.

In my experience, the bankruptcy courts are typically debtor-friendly and want to see debtors improve their financial situation in bankruptcy. Remember, any time a borrower's financial situation improves, it benefits us as secured lienholders, because it means a higher likelihood that borrowers will make on-time payments moving forward after the bankruptcy is discharged or completed.

Bankruptcy can be complicated for the borrower and the borrower's attorney, but from the creditor's perspective, it's relatively straightforward. There are only a couple of filings that creditors are responsible for, and if I don't like the way I am being treated in a bankruptcy plan, I can always have an attorney file an objection on my behalf.

Also, in most cases, the debtor will be making payments to the bankruptcy trustee, a neutral third party that's responsible for reviewing the bankruptcy filings and debtor documents to make sure everything is verified and financially feasible. The trustee also usually receives the monthly payments from the debtor and then disburses to the creditors in conjunction with the approved bankruptcy plan.

If borrowers don't make their required monthly payments, don't provide everything that's required by the court, and/or don't complete their plan, their case is *dismissed,* and they continue to be personally liable for the original debt without any further bankruptcy protection.

Ultimately, only you, your financial advisor, and your attorney can truly see whether mortgage loans in active Chapter 13 bankruptcy are a good fit for you. I highly recommend you first speak with an experienced bankruptcy attorney to verify all your rights and responsibilities as a creditor.

Keep in mind that the numbers for completing a Chapter 13 bankruptcy plan and receiving a discharge are low. Between 2006 and 2017, only 48 percent of those who filed Chapter 13 completed their plan and were discharged.[61]

---

[61]https://www.uscourts.gov/statistics-reports/bapcpa-report-2017#:~:text=A%20total%20of%20318%2C751%20chapter,or%20plan%20completion%20in%202017.&text=In%2048%20percent%20of%20the,from%2052%20percent%20in%202016.

Lien Stripping in Chapter 13

There is one situation in which a Chapter 13 bankruptcy can be dangerous for junior lien mortgage loan investors. This occurs when a debtor can prove that a second, or junior, lien is *wholly unsecured*. This means the collateral property is worth less than the balance of the first lien, with not even one dollar of equity above the first lien.

In this situation, a homeowner filing for bankruptcy can file a motion to remove their second lien. If approved, upon the borrower completing their plan and receiving a discharge, this motion would effectively remove the lien from the property as well as the borrower's personal liability for the debt, thus rendering the lender's investment worthless.

To date, I have never had a borrower obtain a lien strip on a second mortgage. One way to prevent this is to check the home's value and first lien balance to ensure the CLTV is well below 100 percent. The more equity in the property, the less likely a judge will approve a motion to strip the second lien.

Mortgage Loan Funds

Not interested in learning the business of mortgage loan investing, but still interested in profiting from the model? Mortgage investment funds could be a more suitable option. They are even more passive than actively purchasing individual loans, and return similar yields.

These funds pool investor capital in order to purchase much larger quantities of loans, and they usually pay a preferred return to investors, which means the investors receive their returns first, before the manager(s) realize any profit.

Unfortunately, many mortgage loan funds that are allowed to advertise are restricted to only allow *accredited* investors, but there are some funds that can accept *sophisticated* investors.

Accredited Investors

The SEC defines an accredited investor as a person who either has an annual income of $200,000 per year ($300,000 for joint income) for the last two years or a net worth of $1,000,000 or more, excluding the value of their primary residence. Because of their net worth and/or income, the SEC believes these investors are capable of making their own investment decisions, without restriction.

Recent changes to the SEC's definition allow for the inclusion of knowledgeable employees of a fund, spousal equivalents, and certain people with relevant credentials and certification from accredited institutions.[62]

Sophisticated Investors

A sophisticated investor may not meet the accredited investor income/net worth status, but is believed to possess superior knowledge of business and financial matters, enough to weigh the merits and risks of an investment.[63] There are certain types of funds that accept a limited number of sophisticated investors, even though they do not meet the income or net worth requirements to be considered accredited.

---

[62]https://www.sec.gov/news/press-release/2020-191
[63]https://www.sec.gov/fast-answers/answers-rule506htm.html

Qualifying a Fund

It's not just the investor who must qualify for the fund, but the fund that must qualify for the investor. After all, mortgage investment funds hold all the same risks as individual mortgage loan investments, and if they are not properly diversified, vetted, or managed, investors run the same risks of loss as they would investing in individual loans.

It is absolutely crucial that you complete a thorough due diligence review of a mortgage fund before agreeing to invest. Just because a fund manager seems like a nice person does not mean they are a good fund manager.

The following questions are absolutely critical to review with a sponsor during the vetting process. The answers to many of these questions will likely be included in the fund offering documents, so be sure to look there as well. If you have any questions about how to review those documents and identify important information, you should speak directly to the fund manager. It is your money; don't be afraid to ask the tough questions.

Who is/are the fund's manager(s)?
Keep in mind that you are investing in the people even more than the model. I like to see that the leadership has a great depth of knowledge in the field, as well as a successful track record. I always ask the manager how much of their own capital they have invested in the fund. That shows how personally vested they are in the fund's success. Additionally, I strongly recommend doing a background check on the manager(s).

What is the strategy of the fund?

Funds can have many strategies. Some might want to focus on single-family, residential first liens. Others might focus primarily on commercial real estate. Still others could choose nonperforming first or second liens. Investors should generally look for a focused, singular strategy organized by a manager with plenty of related experience. If a fund is going to buy both residential and commercial real estate, performing and nonperforming first and second liens, and anything else that comes along that looks appealing, there may not be enough expertise and focus in one field, which greatly increases the risk. It is very rare that a management team is a market leader in all those fields.

What is the fund's yield?
Most mortgage funds pay investors a preferred return ranging from 8 to 10 percent, depending on the types of assets the fund purchases. The riskier the fund's strategy, the more yield an investor should expect. For example, in my experience, purchasing nonperforming loans is a much riskier investment model than performing loans. I do think there is a place for NPL funds, but I also believe the investors should share a much larger portion of the profit, not just a preferred return, to reflect the risks involved.

When are investors paid?
If an investor is counting on the fund for reliable income, they may want to look for a fund that pays a monthly distribution. Also, make sure to note if there is a delay between when the funds are invested and the preferred return distributions begin.

What fees does the fund charge?

Ideally, a well-run mortgage loan fund will have no fees. Some investment funds, however, charge a management fee of 2 percent or more per year, which is payable to the managers regardless of fund performance. Funds are also known to charge myriad additional administrative and management fees that can really add up and could affect distributions to the investors. A fund **without** fees demonstrates that the sponsors are very confident in their model, because they will not be paid anything for their hard work unless the fund does well.

What costs does the fund incur?
Even if the fund charges a low fee, the costs of running the fund can impact profits and yield. I suggest that investors look for a fund that balances these costs against the cash flows of the fund. If there isn't much of a buffer between the monthly net income and investor-preferred return obligations, the fund could get into trouble down the road, unable to pay its costs and/or investor-preferred returns.

What is the fund's lockup period?
Many commercial real estate funds have a minimum commitment of five to ten years, which means investors may not redeem their shares during that period. A lot can happen in that span of time, so investors should look for funds with as short a required commitment as possible. Once the lockup period has passed, there should be a clear procedure for redeeming shares and exiting the fund.

Does the fund have any broker-dealer affiliations?
A broker-dealer, licensed by FINRA, is in the business of buying and selling securities. While this is not a requirement, a fund's affiliation with a broker-dealer represents an additional measure of confidence, because

broker-dealers complete very rigorous analyses and reviews of fund offerings before recommending them to their clients.

What is the current distribution between first and second liens?

If the fund invests in first liens, investors need to know either their policy for minimum property value or their current average property value. I would be wary of funds that purchase loans or have an average value under $75,000 because lower-value properties have lower-income owners and typically have more problems and higher default rates.

If the fund invests in second liens, I want to know what percent of their loans has a combined loan to value (CLTV) under 100 percent. This answer will tell me how many of their loans have full equity coverage between the first and second lien, which is an additional measure of conservative investing.

In which states do you own loans, and how many loans are owned in each state?

It's critical that investors find funds with adequate geographic diversification. If all the loans are held in one city or state and that area sees a major employer move or a natural disaster, the investors could be in big trouble.

What is the fund's current delinquency rate?

If the strategy of the fund is to invest in performing loans but it has a troubling percentage of loans (more than 5 percent) that are nonperforming, I would be concerned.

What is the fund UPB vs. invested capital?

This is an important liquidity issue that tells investors how much debt the fund owns in relation to the amount of investor capital they have accepted. If the fund were ever to be liquidated, would there be plenty of money left over to pay back investors? The more debt the fund owns in relation to invested capital, the more confident investors can be that the fund could survive a financial downturn or a spike in delinquency.

What are the monthly cash flows of the fund?
This is a measure of the monthly payment income versus its preferred return obligations to investors. The fund should be taking in plenty of excess capital monthly that should be invested in more loans to increase the financial health of the fund and strengthen its safety net.

How high a delinquency rate could the fund withstand in order to still pay preferred returns to borrowers?
Under a preferred return model, the fund managers know exactly what their monthly obligations are to investors. If a catastrophic downturn occurred and 25 percent of a fund's loans became delinquent, could the fund still pay investors? As an investor, I want safety and security more than flashy promises of astronomical returns. After all, the first key to investing is to not lose money.

Has the fund ever missed a payment to investors?
If the fund has, I would want to know why, and what changes have been made to ensure that never happens again.

What are the tax implications of fund participation?
When buying into a fund outside a qualified account, make sure there are no tax surprises, such as managers issuing

capital gains distributions for proceeds from sales within the fund. Additionally, I like to see that the fund has a licensed CPA handling its forms and filings, both with the IRS and investors.

Are there any sales loads?
Ideally, the fund should have no sales loads or commission charges for buying or selling your interests outside of the lockup period.

Choosing between investing in a fund and purchasing individual loans or partials should be a time versus reward consideration. How much better do you think you can do on your own after investing all the time and taking the risks to learn the business and develop a network? Also, are you able to spend the capital to diversify your loan portfolio properly? While an individual investor may only be able to buy five to ten loans at a time, a fund might have three hundred in its inventory, providing a far better hedge against risks.

In my opinion, investing in a mortgage loan fund is really the only totally passive, high-yield, secured real estate investment available.

LIENLORD

Mortgage Loan Investing in Tax-Deferred and Tax-Free Accounts

Whenever an investor wants to amplify the power of their investing capital, a qualified account such as an IRA should be considered. Investing within an IRA allows an investor to enjoy tax-deferred or tax-free growth, and if it is a self-directed IRA, it might be the perfect place for a mortgage loan portfolio.

The Self-Directed IRA

Self-directed, traditional IRAs are tax-deferred accounts offered through select custodians that allow specified alternative and nontraditional investments. Like other traditional IRAs, they have no income limits and often allow investors to deduct all or a portion of their annual contribution. Contribution limits change often, but as of

2020 individuals below age fifty can contribute $6,000 and investors who are fifty and over can contribute $7,000.[64]

Assets grow without taxation in the IRA; then, when the owner begins taking qualified distributions, they are taxable based on the owner's current income.

A self-directed IRA is not, in itself, an investment. It's simply an account that can hold cash and other permissible assets. Custodians for self-directed IRAs will allow the IRA to hold assets like mortgage loan investments, mortgage loan funds, real estate, multifamily buildings, raw land, tax liens, oil and gas, and more. Investors can invest in funds and syndications that pool capital in these investment niches, if they don't feel comfortable or aren't interested in making the individual investment decisions themselves.

If you are self-employed or own a small business, make sure you look into SEP IRA or SIMPLE IRA.

Self-directed IRAs allow more options and flexibility for investors who don't want to turn over 100 percent of their retirement to large companies where they have no control over what happens. There are at least fifty different self-directed IRA custodians that help investors set up these accounts, and they make sure the investments and documentation are compliant with IRS regulations. One thing these custodians cannot do, however, is provide any advice on individual investments.

With potentially higher yields than bonds and bond funds, mortgage loan funds within a self-directed traditional

---

[64]https://www.irs.gov/retirement-plans/retirement-plans-faqs-regarding-iras-contributions#:~:text=The%20annual%20contribution%20limit%20for,your%20filing%20status%20and%20income.

IRA mean investors can enjoy a high-yield, lower-risk investment with deferred taxation—ensuring their growth compounds continually.

Self-Directed Roth IRA

As of the writing of this book in 2020, a lot of focus has been placed on the amount of new debt the government has originated in order to keep the economy afloat during an unprecedented time in our history.

Eventually, this money will need to be paid back.

The majority opinion is that we should prepare for large tax increases, both on income and capital gains, in the coming years. This will make traditional IRAs less advantageous, since tax-deferred IRAs avoid taxes when the money is contributed, but require applicable taxes to be paid later, when the money is distributed from the account.

Roth IRAs, however, are funded with after-tax dollars and qualified distributions are nontaxable. If you believe tax rates will be higher when you are ready to retire, you should strongly consider a Roth IRA.

Roth IRAs do have income and contribution limits that change yearly, so these factors should be discussed with your financial advisor.

The restrictions and disadvantages of buying real estate in an IRA make mortgage loan investments the perfect alternative. If you need a list of self-directed IRA providers who handle mortgage loan investments, feel free to reach out to me.

Backdoor Roth IRA

One of the issues that many investors have with the Roth IRA are the income limits. Those who exceed the annual income limits can still obtain a Roth IRA through a special "backdoor" option.

To use this strategy, you would fund a traditional IRA, which has no income limits. Then, you'd move the money into a Roth IRA using a Roth conversion, paying the applicable taxes up front at the time of conversion.

Keep in mind that Roth conversions are permanent and cannot be reversed once completed. Also, there are many rules that need to be followed for the conversion to be legal, so complete the conversion under the guidance of a custodial bank, financial advisor, or brokerage.

Self-Directed Health Savings Account (HSA)

Impressed by the tax-free growth power of the Roth IRA? Well, it gets even better! To keep health care premiums low, more individuals and families are choosing high-deductible health insurance plans (HDHP) with a coordinating health savings account (HSA). The HSA is designed to pay the expenses of the HDHP until patients meet their deductibles each year.

To encourage these plans, which are also cheaper for employers, the government created generous tax breaks for using HSA accounts. The HSA allows participants the unbelievable benefits of:

- tax-deductible contributions (these change yearly)

- tax-free growth (unused funds can accumulate year after year)
- tax-free withdrawals, as long as the funds are spent on health care–related expenses
- upon reaching age sixty-five, funds can be used for any expense without penalty (with applicable taxes)

The best part of the HSA? The funds contributed to the account can be invested! By opening a self-directed HSA account with a participating custodian, investors can purchase full mortgage loans, funds, or partials in their HSA.

The ultimate goal of a self-directed HSA should be to generate at least enough income from mortgage loan investments to pay the HDHP deductible each year.

LIENLORD

In Conclusion: It's Time to Get Started!

Growing up, my grandfather used to say to me, "It's not what you do in life that you regret. It's what you don't do." Life has given me a lot of challenges, just as it gives everyone. While my path to passive investing has been a little longer, the lessons I've learned the hard way have given me a perspective I hope to share with others.

For me, material possessions can never match freedom. Being rich is not about hitting a certain threshold of income or savings, but simply about having more money coming in each month than you are spending. This is especially easy to achieve when you are able to reinvest gains and cash flow to expand your portfolio, rather than constantly maintaining the assets you've already accumulated.

I know I said earlier that lending is a business, and we should always make our decisions based on the numbers. It's true. But in closing, I'd like to share a story that proves that business and investing aren't always about yield and profit; there are real people on the other side of these loans, and sometimes we have an opportunity to help them in ways that can change their lives.

In 2019 I purchased a pool of eight loans from a large mortgage fund I frequently do business with. One of the loans was on a dilapidated house in Texas. The fund purchased it as part of a large nonperforming pool and completed the foreclosure process. To avoid a foreclosure sale, the borrower filed bankruptcy the day before the foreclosure sale date.

I didn't really want the loan, but the fund pressed me to take it as part of the pool. When I reviewed the loan, I didn't understand why the fund was demanding that the borrower pay back $57,000 on a property that was only worth $40,000. While it was their legal right, it made little practical sense. I could understand the borrower's frustration as I read his attorney's bankruptcy motions.

As I predicted, the borrower's bankruptcy case was dismissed due to his failure to make his payments after the court ruled against his request to have the UPB lowered. I had two choices: schedule a foreclosure sale and most likely receive the deed to the house, or try to work something out with the borrower. I begged the servicer to get ahold of the borrower, but they were unsuccessful. As a last resort, and with the approval of the foreclosure attorney, I sent the borrower a FedEx with a handwritten note asking him to call me. He did.

The borrower, Ed, was a retired veteran somehow surviving on $1,300 a month in disability. He explained that he had already started packing to move, but had nowhere to go. He had lived in the home for thirty years. I could hear his voice shaking on the phone, and honestly, I became emotional too. I could tell that Ed had lived a hard life and was devastated about the possibility of losing his home.

I asked him what he could afford, and he volunteered $500 per month. You know when you speak to someone on the phone and you instantly know they are telling the truth? Shocked at his honesty, I told Ed that I wanted to modify his loan to lower the payment to only $250 per month, and his loan balance all the way to $30,000, the amount he argued for in his bankruptcy filing.

Not only did he agree, he was ecstatic, insisting on making the payment via ACH on the first of each month. He seemed incredulous that this was actually happening, and I could hear that he was choking up knowing that he could stay in his home. I had a huge smile on my face as we spoke. I told him I would have the servicer ship the documents to modify his loan. He thanked me countless times, and we hung up. The feeling I received from that phone call lasted for weeks afterward.

Guess what happened? Ed has made his $250 payment on the first of every month since our conversation, taking this investment from a potential loss with a displaced borrower to a positive yield. I doubt I will ever speak to Ed again, but I'll never forget his story. I wish him the best and hope more lenders take the time to review each loan with a pragmatic mindset.

Investors don't need to be tough, and neither does investing. Don't feel limited to traditional investments that are convoluted and unpredictable. A stable 9 percent yield can beat the volatility of the stock market's average annual return of 10 percent *every time*. Take control of a portion of your investments and place them into a simple alternative that all investors can understand. At any stage of your life, I firmly believe that high-yield cash flow should be your focus.

I made a mistake by getting involved in direct-ownership real estate investment and went too long thinking that the difficult path of a landlord was as good as it would get. Real estate wasn't the problem—it was the active nature of real estate investing. Had my emphasis from the start been on passive investments, I would have been able to grow my portfolio continuously *and* enjoy my life. The returns have worked out to be the same.

My goal in writing this book was simply to get you to consider an alternative investment that has been very powerful for me, but I'd like to challenge you, as an investor and a person, to take action after reading this book. Keep investigating, keep researching, and at some point, take informed, advisor-reviewed action—and have no regrets.

Feel free to contact me with any questions or for more information about mortgage loan investing.

Eric Scharaga
www.ericscharaga.com
eric@damencapital.com
847-222-8888

Acknowledgments

Although I taught authors for twenty-three years, I never considered becoming one. This experience, during the infamous summer of 2020, has taught me how to become comfortable with frustration. Countless afternoons I sat on my back porch, sweating in the heat and shaking my head because I knew I had to rewrite the conclusion yet again. I hope I finally got it right.

I must thank several people for their brilliance, kindness, and patience with me while I learned this business. Your influence is woven page by page into this book.

Josh, my mentor and good friend, thank you for teaching me so much over the years, so much more than just mere investing. You took a chance on me when I was a desperate real estate investor and encouraged me to finally take that leap into the great unknown. You were right.

Evan, hopefully it wasn't too obvious that I was a novice buyer. Thank you for guiding me through so many tough files and always answering my endless emails within minutes. Everything worked out just fine.

Thank you to all my friends who encouraged me not to quit early on during the writing process. I owe a special thank you to Ken, Tom, Roberto, Lou, and Steve for agreeing to read this book in its beta form and providing honest feedback and encouragement.

Finally, Sara, you were the only person who believed in me and stood by my side when everyone else thought I was crazy. Thank you.

Glossary

Accredited investor: Investor that is allowed to purchase securities by satisfying SEC requirements regarding their income, net worth, and/or professional experience.

Amortizing mortgage loan: Mortgage loan that requires scheduled payments of principal and interest, with the majority of the interest paid at the beginning of the loan.

Arrears: Unpaid interest during a period of mortgage loan default.

Assignment of mortgage/deed of trust (AOM): Recorded document that transfers ownership interest of a lien to a subsequent lender.

Allonge: Paper attached to a promissory note that transfers ownership of the note to a new lender.

Allonge chain: All of the endorsements/allonges required to transfer the note from the original lender through to the current lender.

AOM chain: All of the mortgages/deeds of trust required to transfer ownership of the lien from the original lender through to the current lender.

Automated Valuation Model (AVM): A sophisticated modeling software that determines property values by combining property data with recent sales transactions.

Balloon payment: A one-time payment required to fully pay off a mortgage prior to its full amortization.

Bankruptcy: Legal process through which individuals or entities who cannot repay debts to creditors may seek relief from some or all their debts.

Bankruptcy discharge: Upon completion of a bankruptcy case, an order that releases the debtor from personal liability for certain specified types of debts.

Bankruptcy dismissal: An order prior to bankruptcy discharge that closes the bankruptcy case without any legal protections for the debtor.

Bankruptcy lien strip: A bankruptcy filing that eliminates a junior lien without equity.

Bankruptcy trustee: Party responsible for overseeing the debtor's estate in a bankruptcy case.

Borrower: The party who pays back a mortgage loan in equal installments in accordance with the promissory note.

Broker Price Opinion (BPO): The estimated value of a property as determined by a real estate broker or other qualified individual or firm.

Cherry picking: An industry term for bidding on individual loans of an investor's choice versus purchasing an entire pool.

Collateral custodian: Business that handles all mortgage loan collateral–related needs for investors.

LIENLORD

Collateral file: All the required documents relating to a mortgage loan.

Collateral property: The property that the lien is filed against and pledged by the borrower as security for a mortgage loan.

Creditor: A bankruptcy term for the party that is owed money.

Cutoff date: The date after which all borrower payments will belong to the purchaser of a mortgage loan.

Debtor: A bankruptcy term for the party who owes money.

Deed: Legal instrument used to transfer property ownership from the old owner to the new owner.

Deed in lieu of foreclosure: An agreement in which a borrower agrees to transfer ownership of a property to the lender in exchange for dismissal of a foreclosure action.

Deed of trust: A recorded instrument securing a loan to the collateral and used mainly in nonjudicial foreclosure states.

Default: Occurs when a borrower stops making required payments on a mortgage loan.

Deferred balance: Usually occurring in a loan mod, the postponement of a portion of a loan balance to a later date and without any regularly scheduled monthly payments.

Discount: A mortgage loan sale price for less than the full UPB.

Due diligence: The steps taken by an investor to determine whether a mortgage loan is a proper investment.

Endorsement: A stamp on the original promissory note that is used to transfer ownership of the instrument to a new lender.

Equity: The current value of a property minus any debt owed by the owner.

Escrowee: A third party used to oversee a mortgage loan purchase between parties.

Estoppel affidavit: Typically used for self-serviced loans; a notarized statement from the borrower agreeing to certain stated loan terms, usually the UPB.

Financial calculator: A specialized calculator used to calculate yield to maturity.

Financial institution: A banking entity that lends depositor funds to borrowers.

First lien: The mortgage recorded first; retains right to first priority for payoff.

Forbearance agreement: A short-term agreement that allows a borrower to temporarily pause or reduce their payments during a time of hardship.

Forced-placed insurance policy: An insurance policy placed by a lender when the property owners' insurance is canceled or has lapsed.

Foreclosure: A legal process in which a lender attempts to recover the balance of a loan from a borrower who has stopped making payments to the lender by forcing the sale of the asset used as the collateral for the loan.

Funding date: In an LSA, the date that the funds are due to the seller.

Health Savings Account (HSA): A tax-advantaged medical savings account available to individuals who are enrolled in a high-deductible health care plan.

Home Equity Line of Credit (HELOC): Usually a junior lien mortgage in which the lender provides a mortgage loan and the collateral is the borrower's equity in their house.

Indicative bid: An initial bid placed by an investor on a mortgage loan subject to certain conditions.

Individual Retirement Account (IRA): A tax-advantaged account designed for retirement savings.

Interest rate: A fee charged by a lender in exchange for a loan, usually payable in installments.

Investment to value (ITV): The amount of money invested by an investor to purchase a mortgage loan, divided by the value of the property.

Judicial foreclosure: A foreclosure action required to go through the court system.

Lender: An individual or business that lends money.

Lender's title policy: A policy that protects the lender from problems or claims against a property's title.

Lien: Provides a lender a legal claim on a property until a debt is paid off.

Loan modification: A written agreement that changes the original terms of a mortgage contract agreed to by the lender and borrower.

Loan sale agreement (LSA): The formal contract used to sell a mortgage loan between parties.

Loan servicer: Private company that collects payments and handles administrative responsibilities required for a mortgage loan in exchange for a fee.

Loan to value (LTV): The amount of money owed by a borrower, divided by the value of the property.

Lost note affidavit: An affidavit filed to justify the loss or destruction of a note secured by a deed of trust or mortgage.

Maturity date: The date on which the final payment is due on a mortgage loan.

Mortgage: A recorded instrument securing a loan to the collateral and used mainly in judicial foreclosure states.

Nonjudicial foreclosure: A foreclosure action that is not required to go through the court system.

Nonperforming loans (NPLs): Mortgage loans that have gone at least ninety days without payment.

Notarization: The witnessing of a legal signature by a licensed third party.

Owner occupied: A property that is a borrower's primary residence.

Par: A mortgage loan sale price for 100 percent of the UPB.

Partial loan purchase: The sale from an existing mortgage loan of a specified number of payments at a specified yield to a third-party investor.

Pay history: A servicing record used to verify the existing balance and monthly and late payments for a mortgage loan account.

Performing loan: A mortgage loan that is current and in good standing with its lender.

Primary residence: The dwelling where a borrower personally lives the majority of the time.

Principal: The amount of debt a borrower owes; also a noninterest portion of a monthly mortgage loan payment.

Promissory note (note): A legal instrument in which a borrower promises in writing to repay a loan under specific terms.

Reperforming loans (RPL): Loans that were previously delinquent but have resumed performing status, frequently under modified terms.

Representations and warranties: In an LSA, statements and promises of good faith from a seller to a buyer.

Roth IRA: Type of IRA in which deposits are made from post-tax income, in which future growth is tax-free.

Schedule A: An addendum to the LSA listing the loans being sold and their individual data, including UPB.

Second lien (junior lien): The mortgage recorded second; retains right to second priority for payoff.

Secondary market: The market in which whole mortgage loans are sold after origination.

Secured creditor: A bankruptcy term for a creditor whose loan is guaranteed by some form of collateral.

Secured loan: A loan in which collateral is promised to guarantee the repayment of the loan.

Self-directed IRA: An individual retirement account that allows alternative investments for retirement savings.

Self-servicing: A mortgage loan that is serviced by an individual investor; not recommended.

Seller financing: A loan provided by the seller of a property to the purchaser.

Servicing transfer: The process of transitioning a loan between servicers in accordance with applicable state and federal laws.

Sophisticated investor: An investor who is deemed to have sufficient experience and industry knowledge to understand an investment offering.

Tape: An industry term for a spreadsheet that contains data on mortgage loans for sale.

Title report: A researched document that outlines the legal status of a property and related information on its ownership.

Traditional IRA: Type of IRA in which taxes are deferred until the funds are accessed in retirement.

Underwrite: Formal steps taken to determine the risk profile of a loan.

Unpaid Principal Balance (UPB): The portion of a mortgage loan at a certain point in time that has not yet been repaid to the lender.

Unsecured loan: Loan issued only based on the borrower's credit worthiness, without any collateral.

LIENLORD

Whole loan: An individual loan issued to a borrower in which the lender retains 100 percent ownership interest in the debt owed.

Yield: An investor's annual return over the life of an investment.

About the Author

Eric Scharaga is the founder of Damen Capital Management, an investment firm that purchases residential mortgage loans nationwide.

Before focusing full-time on mortgage loan investing, Eric worked for twenty-three years as a public high school teacher. In 2001, after reading *Rich Dad, Poor Dad*, he began investing in rental properties, with the dream of leaving his job to become an investor.

Unfortunately, after thirteen years dealing with the constant stresses and unpredictability of landlording, he came to the realization that he would never achieve his goal of financial freedom through rental properties. He found the business of landlording even more volatile than the stock market, and developed a strong understanding that most investors should not invest in their own rental properties.

In 2016, while still teaching, Eric transitioned to the more stable and passive cash flow of mortgage loan investing, which ultimately allowed him to leave his full-time job in 2019. Since 2016 he has purchased over 250 loans exceeding $2 million in purchase price.

In his book, *Lienlord*, Eric gives an introduction to the power of investing like a bank in owner-occupied mortgage loans. He resides in the suburbs of Chicago with his wife and two children and is passionate about personal finance and financial freedom. His goal is to continue introducing investors across the county to the power of reliable investment yields.

Feel free to contact me with any questions or for more information about mortgage loan investing.

Eric Scharaga
www.ericscharaga.com
eric@damencapital.com
847-222-8888